And suddenly happiness of being

what I know for sure

entered me.

Kindness

Being in Balance

THE VISION BOARD

THE VISION BOARD

THE SECRET TO AN EXTRAORDINARY LIFE

Joyce Schwarz

COLLINS DESIGN
An Imprint of HarperCollins Publishers

THE VISION BOARD: THE SECRET TO AN EXTRAORDINARY LIFE

HarperCollins books may be purchased for educational, business, or sales promotional use. For information, please write: Special Markets Department, HarperCollins*Publishers,* 10 East 53rd Street, New York, NY 10022.

First published in 2008 by
Collins Design
An Imprint of HarperCollins*Publishers*
10 East 53rd Street
New York, NY 10022
Tel: (212) 207-7000
Fax: (212) 207-7654
collinsdesign@harpercollins.com
www.harpercollins.com

Distributed throughout the world by
HarperCollins*Publishers*
10 East 53rd Street
New York, NY 10022
Fax: (212) 207-7654

Design and Production by The Stonesong Press and Sophia Latto

Library of Congress Control Number: 2008935075
ISBN: 978-0-06-195638-6

Printed in China
First Paperback Printing, 2009

Opening vision board and back cover art by Katy Taylor.
Vision board on preceding page by Donna Factor.

Hundreds of artists submitted their art for The Vision Board *book by Joyce Schwarz.*
We thank all of the artists and contributors from the USA and around the world.
Share your vision at www.ihaveavision.org.

Table of Contents

Foreword

Vision boards are one of the most powerful ways to visualize your goals and keep you focused. If you have been setting goals or studying my materials on goal-setting, chances are you have started, or want to create, a vision board.

After all, just like Hollywood directors use storyboards to map out their blockbuster films, you can now create a vision board that, like the lens of a new HD camera, focuses close-up on you as the star—not the extra—in your own extraordinary life story.

Everything that's coming into your life you are attracting into your life. And it's attracted by virtue of the images you're holding in your mind. It's what you're thinking. Whatever is going on in your mind you are attracting to you. Your vision board reinforces your positive images and enables you to attract the best possible in life. The images you plant in your mind instantly set up an attractive force, which governs the results in your life. Vision is the key connector between one's daily goals and one's lifetime purpose.

"Most people are extras in their own movie."

—**Bob Proctor**

It's my pleasure to write the foreword to *The Vision Board*, an invaluable guide in your visioning process. This very informative and easy-to-follow guide finally takes the mystery out of the vision board creation process and opens the way for you to practice the law of attraction as you ask, believe, and receive your visions.

I recommend using a vision board more than any other method of visualization. It's an excellent method for helping you attract the good you desire—in all areas of your life.

Remember, most people are not going after what they want; even some of the most serious goal seekers and goal setters go after what they think they can get.

To live an extraordinary life, you've got to develop mental strength. And you develop mental strength with will. The will is the mental faculty that gives you the ability to hold one idea on the screen of your mind to the exclusion of all outside distractions. Joyce tells the story of my clients the Shroyer family in the "Your Personal Vision Statement" chapter and for them only a vision wall would do.

Your vision board is intended to inspire you and focus you on your goals by keeping them on display 24/7 . . . 365 days of the year. Committed people like you who want to attract the happiness they deserve in their lives are discovering that a vision board is an essential law of attraction tool. Even the most powerful person deals with ups and downs, but a great vision board enables you to stay positive, which attracts more positive things and people and enables you to create an extraordinary life. Your vision board keeps your *why* right in front of you—focusing you on the big picture of your life!

This book and its messages from my friends from the movie and the book *The Secret* and my colleagues in personal development and other prominent leaders in sports, Hollywood, public service, as well as everyday people, will inspire you to focus, achieve your goals using inspired action, and live an extraordinary life.

All of the great achievers of the past have been visionary figures; they were men and women who projected into the future. They thought of what could be, rather than what already was, and then they moved themselves into action to bring these things into fruition.

Throughout these chapters you'll discover how your vision is invaluable in this life success process. If you can conceive it in your mind, then it can be brought to the physical world. Take the first step in predicting your own successful future. Build a mental picture of exactly how you would like to live.

Make a firm decision to hold on to that vision and positive ways to improve everything will begin to flow into your mind. Reinforce these mental images with the power words, affirmations, and pictures on your vision board.

Don't worry about how you will do it or where the resources will come from. Your job is the *what!* Make sure to power your decision with enthusiasm and recharge it daily by focusing on the visions on your board. Refuse to worry about how it will happen.

The Vision Board holds the key to helping you create your own vision for each area of your life, enabling you to tap into the ultimate power of visualization. Using your own mental image power—more advanced than any Hollywood visual effects software—freeze-frame your vision with intention and activate it with decision. Become the star in the movie of your life. Start today! It's time for you to see your goals and yourself in a close-up of your best possible you. Open these pages and begin your opportunity of a lifetime to attract abundance, prosperity, and love.

—Bob Proctor,
Author of the best-selling book, *You Were Born Rich*

Introduction

As you open this book and begin your journey, the most important advice I can share with you is that your time is *now*. No matter what your circumstances—whether you are recently divorced or you have just been laid off from your job, or you are happy in your life but yearn for something more—you can bring positive change to your life. This is not a magical, mystical guide to the mantra that makes it all better or all okay. But it is an inside look at how thousands of my clients from all walks of life use specific principles to change paths, to get back on track, and to create the futures they desire. How they use some of the most powerful personal development tools, techniques, and strategies available will be presented. These tools, techniques, and strategies are grounded in the law of attraction—that you attract everything into your life through your thoughts and actions. You'll learn about my version—GRABS—and how the mindset that results enables you to achieve your goals.

You've probably already experienced a bit of these techniques anyway. Perhaps you discounted the results by touting them as "luck," "miracles," one-time answers to prayers, or just being in the right place at the right time. Those moments are just tastes of what this book is about and how you can harness this power. Please note this is not a religious book, but it does explore the mind-body-spirit relationship and how your inner insight and intention lead to manifesting your visions in the outer world.

Vision Boards

This book focuses on a deceptively simple yet powerful tool called a vision board, a physical, visual manifestation of the change you want to bring to your life. The book starts by unveiling the science and spirit of a little-known practice called visioning and reveals the craft of creating your own personal vision statement that leads to the creation of vision boards.

You'll do exercises that help you focus on the positive aspects of your life and on what you want, and you'll read anecdotes from today's top personal development leaders and visionaries. The bottom line is you do deserve to live your best possible life. You can change your mind and change your life to live the dreams you once only imagined! You are not a victim or a martyr. You just need to believe that real change is possible—that an extraordinary life of fulfillment is within reach.

Seeing Dreams Come True

This book is about today, it's about now—it's about real people who have brought remarkable change to their lives with powerful, real dreams and visions. It's not about wishful thinking. People from all walks of life—whose inspiring stories are shared here—have the same goal: to see their dreams come true and share their legacy of opportunity with the world. They did this through the techniques provided in this book.

Now is the time for you to suspend your disbelief—to believe that anything is possible in your life—and to embrace change. Be brave and take the leap—what comes next will amaze you.

Unfettered freedom and the ability to fly as high as the sky is a universal dream that artist Mai-Liis Chaska Peacock expresses in her vision mini-quilt called Peace. The richness of the colors and the charm of the doll adds a warmth to this design that shows you can express your vision in many different mediums—perfect for reminding us of the joy of childlike wonder in our own lives.

VISIONING

Visioning is a self-exploration process that may be unfamiliar to many readers, and it is one of the most valuable techniques and strategies presented in this book. It is well known in the law of attraction community, with versions of the experience now spreading into other arenas of life and personal development. It is sometimes compared to a combination of "soul-searching" and meditation, and even incorporates improvisation techniques.

Visioning is a group-focused activity that allows you to gather information and get input from other people. Life coaches, career strategists, and such economic development groups as VISTA, the United Nations, and the World Bank use variations of the visioning process. It is used in scenario creation and in model development by religious and educational communities and even in the business world of entrepreneurship and corporate planning.

Rochelle Schofield's colorful self-portrait collage board reflects the inner wisdom gained from her past, including her work as a fashion designer, and her successful marriage—going on twenty-two years—to Hollywood producer John D. Schofield. The defining images flow together in tribute to her African American heritage.

Your vision will become clear only when you can look into your own heart…. Who looks outside, dreams; who looks inside, awakes.

—Carl Jung

I recommend that my clients make time for a visioning experience prior to creating their first vision boards. Here's how it can help:

✦ It clears the cobwebs of uncertainty or confusion about what you want.

✦ It fosters new perspectives about your opportunities.

✦ It provides a virtual doorway where you can leave the past behind and enter into your future *now*, not tomorrow.

✦ It gives you a system or ritual that you can latch on to as a way to "re-vision" or update your dreams, wishes, and desires periodically when you get stuck.

✦ It is a great option for dealing with "trouble at the border" when you are about to go through a rite of passage, such as moving from being single to being in a committed relationship or marriage, and are still wondering how to do this successfully.

The World Bank (left) *and the United Nations use personal visioning exercises to encourage people in third-world countries to express their own visions for the future.*

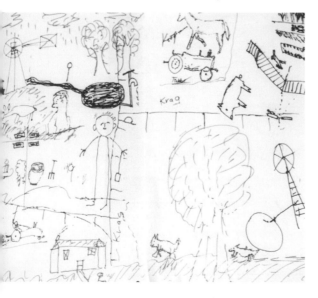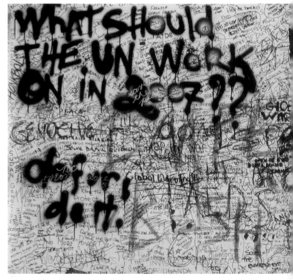

Visioning Illuminated

Michael Bernard Beckwith, founder and spiritual director of the Agape International Spiritual Center in Los Angeles, California, is credited as being an originator of the visioning process. He says, "Visioning is an inner spiritual practice by which we train ourselves to intuit the Spirit's vision for our life in areas such as our spiritual evolution, profession, relationships, and creative expression. It is catching the unique way in which we are intended to deliver our gifts, talents, and skills on the planet."

Beckwith explains that there is a bigger pattern of life beyond that which we experience with the five senses. "This awareness shifted my perception tremendously, and the Life Visioning Process developed as a way of applying that new insight to the founding and expansion of Agape International and all areas of my life."

During a visioning session, I advise my clients to focus on key words that are expressed by them or, if they are working with a group, by the members of

Don't we all want to find our place here? Michelle Oravitz, the artist of this vision board, provides what she calls a one-size-fits-all affirmation—"I am fulfilling my divine purpose in life"—the one phrase that we can all share before, during, and after our visioning experiences.

the group. Be sure to explore not just what is safe, but what you really love to do in life. Delve into what you have not dared to do full time, like a hobby or an avocation such as sailing or adventure travel.

Stages of Visioning

There are several different stages in the visioning process: At first, a deep sense that we're surrounded by unconditional love. Then, a transition into conscious awareness—that we live, move, and have our being in this unconditional love, and we open ourselves up to what that love feels like.

Bob Proctor promises that if you "fall in love with an idea, you'll be guided by an unseen hand in the right direction and everything will fall into place." After all, this is your life. No matter how outrageous the insight from your visioning exercise appears at first glance, flow with it.

Why do you need a vision for your life? Beckwith says, "People who have no vision for their lives are sleepwalking without a hint as to why they are here or what their purpose is. They are drifting along on the currents of the culture's conditioned collective beliefs without discerning for themselves whether those beliefs are harmful or beneficial, progressive or regressive."

What's the difference between your life purpose and your vision? Beckwith teaches that our purpose on this planet is to be the highest expression of love possible. "Anyone who has made a breakthrough into fourth-dimensional living or has had a near-death experience or a mystical realization knows this. The highest vision for our life is a living fire at our deepest core waiting to emerge as our own unique love-expression as a beneficial presence on the planet. It is our delivery system." We are multidimensional, multifaceted beings who have primary visions to catch or open up to.

We are all spiritual beings made in the image and likeness of pure Spirit. Each of us is a composite spiritual idea containing every idea that infinite Mind has ever thought. When we begin to understand our purpose for being here, which is to be a revealer of love, then we can start to open ourselves up to a greater vision for us and to discover our own unique way to deliver that love—the individual mechanism by which we can express that love.

Created by healer Jennifer McLean, this board expresses positive affirmations and hints at her techniques for clearing old, unwanted beliefs and thoughts that limit her potential. Through the visioning process you'll discover some of your own positive affirmations and will want to begin to focus on new beliefs and leave the past behind.

Be aware of the spiritual feeling that develops, sometimes described as a sense of "stillness," a clearing of the mind and an opening of the heart. (People actually feel sensations like their sinuses opening and their hearts beating slower.) According to Beckwith, "Recognizing and trusting the inner intuitive feeling tone is the very foundation of visioning."

A Visioning Frame of Mind

Pause and wait as first you inwardly start to hear, see, and catch what is intuitively coming to you. Focus on what it looks like, what it feels and sounds like. Pay attention to any symbols or metaphors that appear in your mind or are mentioned in the discussion by the other participants. Be sure to do all of this without judgment. Keep yourself open to whatever comes up or is expressed.

The Difference between Visioning and Visualization

Visioning differs dramatically from visualization. Visioning is a process where your soul reveals your heart's desires, prompted by a circle of like-minded supporters who add their own insights. Traditionally, visioning is a group process. It helps you find a direction in life. Visualization is more often an individual technique where you picture a desired outcome or goal. A marathoner may visualize an entire course, along with the moment of "crashing" through the banner at the finish line; you might see yourself being thin so that you almost self-hypnotize yourself into feeling thin.

Once you write down these thoughts or record them in audio or video format, you'll want to be prepared to discuss how the findings feel to you, both emotionally and spiritually.

The whole visioning cycle depends upon an understanding that you go into the exercise with a willingness to make necessary changes. Beckwith explains, "Visioning is a potent tool for self-transformation because it aligns us with the evolutionary impulse seeking expression through and as us. And this process goes on throughout eternity."

While Beckwith's approach is directed at self-transformation and authentic self-expression, other wisdom leaders focus on the power of manifestation or self-empowerment. If you read *The Secret* or saw the movie, you are aware that the law of attraction tells us that like attracts like.

Bob Proctor explains that "everything that's coming into your life you are attracting into your life. And it's attracted to you by virtue of the images you're holding in your mind. It's what you're thinking. You are attracting whatever is going on in your mind."

The Journey Home

wake up!

Living An Awakened Life

The Language of the Soul

Visioning isn't a time for daydreaming or reverie. It is an exercise in awakening your inner spirit. Here, artist Katy Taylor, an Interfaith Minister, encourages us with her own vision board collage to "wake up" to the language of the soul, to journey to our inner home and live an awakened life—so appropriate as a way to encourage you to plan your own visioning session now.

Visioning Tips

Here are some ways to make sure you capture all of the wisdom that evolves from the words expressed and comments revealed during your visioning work. (Visioning sessions can run from one hour to a day or even fill a weekend.)

✦ Write down every word or picture described to you by your visioning group or that comes to you just before, during, or after the session.

✦ During a post-session summary, weave together images and phrases that link together naturally; for example, set up sections in your summary to highlight locales mentioned by city, state, or country or by physical description, such as mountains, lakes, oceans, or beaches. By weaving the findings of your visioning session together, you will get a bigger picture of not only your life's purpose but also how to create a vision statement that further narrows this information into a clear and concise sentence or phrase you can easily remember and use for inspiration.

The Importance of GRABS

In the movie and the book *The Secret*, the basic system for creation is a three-part sequence of Ask, Believe, and Receive. Your role is to ask the universe for what you want and to be as specific as possible. In the second step, believe, your responsibility is to believe that you have already received it. Dr. Beckwith further clarifies that it's not enough to simply intellectually believe that that which you seek has already been given; rather, you must imbue your consciousness with a corresponding feeling-tone of conviction about your deservedness and the self-givingness of the universe. In order to receive, the third part, you have to feel good and be on the frequency of receiving. You want to generate the feelings of having what you asked for now.

Based on my years of experience, I've put my own spin on the sequence. I call it **GRABS**.

> **G** stands for **gratitude**
> **R** for **release** and **receive**
> **A** for **acknowledge** and **ask**
> **B** for **be** and **believe**
> **S** for **share**

How GRABS Works

Always start with **gratitude**—it precedes any action. Being grateful for life itself, breathing deeply, and saying your gratitudes each day and along the way are essential. **Releasing** the old ideas and thoughts about yourself and being receptive to **receiving** the "new" are essential. From the moment you open your mind, be prepared to **receive** change and new opportunity. Be ready to receive now, not just tomorrow. **Acknowledge** your progress and achievements and your very being; and **ask** for guidance for the right path to realizing your goals and vision. Ask for the things you want as specifically as possible. **Be** yourself—be as authentic to the real you as you can using the new knowledge and insight you discover in your visioning process, during the creation of your vision statement, and during the vision board creation exercise itself; and **believe** with such strong conviction that you know your dreams will manifest. Believe that anything and everything is possible. Don't ask how, don't ask if you are deserving, don't question why you versus someone else. Finally, **share** the bounty received. Abundance should be shared. This will increase the power of change in your life and inspire others. Help others be grateful, give to them, and you'll receive in return. Be assured that by sharing you are seeding your own harvest in return.

GRABS and Visioning

Begin your visioning session with an expression of **gratitude**, be ready to **release** the old ideas and **receive** wisdom and insight, and even the wants you know already. **Acknowledge** your progress and **ask** for what you want; at the same time **be** yourself and **believe** you have already received everything you ask for. Then **share** your abundance of insight and gifts, which brings more gratitude into your own life. This cycle will propel you forward.

Antenna Up—Quantum Leap Ahead: Manifesting Your Vision

Most of the wisdom leaders talk about taking baby steps along the way to your vision. However, I encourage you to be prepared to take a quantum leap (like a long jump in life) that defies gravity or other rules. Many of the vision board artists in this book embraced what I call quantum leaps of opportunity to realize their visions. Instead of going along step by step, you can grab on to a rope and swing across the valley ahead or grab a rope lift instead of climbing up the mountain. Be prepared for your own quantum leap. Although the sequence of GRABS provides a stepping stone to your vision of your life, the antenna analogy is very appropriate in working with the law of attraction because it's said that the law works a bit like a radio station that is broadcasting a frequency that you can almost hear and feel—a type of energy described in quantum physics that makes us all connected together in a sense of oneness.

Mind the What, Not the How: Over and over as a practitioner of the law of attraction, it's crucial to remember that your part is the *what*, not the *how*.

The Who of the How: One of the wonderful wonders that the world has revealed to me is that often the *how* comes from a *who!* What do I mean? The answer to *how* is meeting or knowing the right person from whom to seek or accept advice or guidance. Here's an example from my life.

After a successful stint in Hawaii as the vice president for the largest ad agency in the Pacific, I took a much-needed break to discover what was next in my life. Through a process not unlike the visioning exercise described in this chapter, I developed a strong intention to go back to college and get a graduate degree in film. I decided to enroll in the American Film Institute's prestigious film production program in Los Angeles. I made an appointment with the director via phone and mail. When I arrived at the AFI office on the day of my interview, the place was empty. A janitor came by and told me the office was closed. As I headed dejectedly to my car, I saw a woman going up the stairs. I asked her where everyone was. She said the office was being remodeled. I told her who I was there to see and she said come back in ten days. I drove back to my hotel with tears steaming down my face. I had flown there from Hawaii and had a letter in my hand with the date and time of my appointment. It was signed by the guy himself.

On the way to the hotel, I stopped at a place called Bagel Nosh in Beverly Hills. I was dressed in my best interview clothes. I walked in, sat at the counter, and ordered a soda. A friendly looking older gentleman with a long beard was sitting next to me and asked what was up. So I told him the whole story. He slapped his hand on the counter and said, "You want to go to film school?" I said, "Yes, that's the goal." "That's easy," he replied. He told me to write down a number, and gave me his name. He said the USC School of Cinematic Arts was the best. I asked him how I was supposed to get in. He told me to call the number and ask for Jim Regan. "Tell him you're a friend of mine."

I made the call and got an appointment to meet Jim Regan later that afternoon. After a brief meeting, during which we realized we both went to Ohio University, Regan asked me if I had my checkbook. I said yes. He signed some papers with a flourish and sent me off to Admissions to enroll.

Less than three hours after standing dejectedly on the AFI stairs I was saying hello to a new life. Someone led me to the how! Unfortunately I lost the guy with the beard's name, but a belated thanks to him for being my *who* that day!

Inspired Action

While the GRABS acronym makes the process easier to remember, it also implies a sense of "inspired action." One of the teachers in *The Secret*, Joe Vitale, says inspired action is any action you take based on an inside nudge; for example, when you suddenly get a desire to drive to the store. You may have no idea why you need to go to the store at that moment. But something within you is urging you out the door. Follow that hunch. It may lead you to your goal. At the store, you may meet the right person, find the right product, or pick up the right magazine that will lead you to completing your dream. I also like to think of it as embracing uncertainty in an almost gamelike fashion, welcoming not fearing it.

Ben Mandel is a longtime client and a true Renaissance man, successfully living out his visions. He is the producer and star of PBS's The New Home Show. *His vision board is a tribute to living out his current vision of becoming a jet pilot; he's working on his license.*

The Spiritual Side of Visioning

Recently, I conducted an interview with Reverend Cynthia James, who learned visioning from Michael Bernard Beckwith.

For her, visioning is a process by which we hear, feel, see, and open ourselves to a spirit, higher power, or creative source. We listen for a plan for any particular project we are working on. She detailed some of the elements behind the practice of visioning, including:

+ sensing into a Divine Idea (or for that thing for which we vision) that is so wonderful it is beyond our imagination;

+ opening the way for that which is unlimited to come into view— into our experience of life;

+ volunteering ourselves as a place in consciousness that is available to allow the perfection and wholeness of the One Life to become manifest;

and

+ becoming a space of deep listening able to hear a spirit's highest vision or idea.

Here are Reverend Cynthia's insightful answers to some questions about the visioning process.

Q: What's the difference between visualization and visioning in the vision board creation process?

A: Visualization creates an in-state scenario—you take visuals and put them on a vision board and see them daily. In visioning, you become a space of deep listening, so that you are available to hear a spirit's idea for a particular project or for your life.

Q: What's the advantage of visioning prior to creating a vision board?

A: It allows you to become quiet or still and get beyond what you know intellectually.

Q: When does one do visioning?

A: You don't do visioning once. It is something that works over a period of time... during which you capture the themes that keep coming up. They become points of reference for your vision board or next steps even after you do your boards. It's good to keep doing visioning.

Q: You mentioned "re-visioning" to me. Is it good to re-vision throughout the year? And not just when we make our first boards?

A: Yes. For example, to this day Dr. Michael, his staff, and his spiritual community conduct visioning sessions to catch the ever-evolving vision for the Agape Movement.

Q: Can you give us an example of when you used visioning with a group and found it valuable?

A: When United Centers for Spiritual Living was getting ready to move our corporate offices to Denver, we started visioning. And what was amazing was that over and over different groups who were involved with the visioning process were visioning some of the same themes: trees, wood, glass, mountains, snow, water. Mountains, trees, wood, and glass surround the building that we found here. At the end of the driveway to the parking lot there is a street sign that reads VISIONLAND.

Q: What are some of the questions to ask during a visioning session?

A: What's the highest vision—the highest level—you can see for my life or my project? What do I need to become for my project to unfold? What must be embraced? What are the next steps? What are the divine ideas that want to be revealed? You can also focus on each individual in the group: What is the highest vision for Mary's life? What is the highest vision for Steve's life?

Q: What happens during a visioning session?

A: Visioning isn't linear; colors and words and feelings and tones will emerge and evolve. You want people to share their thoughts so that by putting them on the board or capturing them in a journal you continue to "feed the field." You want to be in high consciousness and align so that you become a container to hold the vision for you or others.

How Does a Visioning Session Work?

In setting up and doing visioning workshops for my clients, I advise them to be ready to release old beliefs about the world and themselves and receive insight and advice and symbols and actual phrases that pop into their heads. The goal of a visioning session is to capture recurring themes, actual phrases, and suggestions that may inspire you not only in the creation of your vision board but also in the next steps of your life experience. If you prefer to re-create the process alone, try the "Passport to Possibility" activity (page 16).

Here's an overview of the basic visioning process:

✦ Gather a group of people together in a quiet room.

✦ Have a facilitator or trained visioning practitioner, if there is one in your area (see Resources for more details), run the session.

- Start with an exercise of gratitude for being there and for the life you have.

- Have the facilitator/practitioner prepare a series of open-ended questions or prompts to spur the process.

- Provide each person in the group with a pencil and paper or another method to document the information, thoughts, ideas, and themes that they perceive when they think about these questions or prompts. After the questions are asked, the facilitator/practitioner asks people involved to share what they "received" during the visioning process.

It is helpful to have a whiteboard or other method to capture the "visions." Some groups prefer to use a master "vision" journal that is added to during future visioning sessions.

Visioning Is an Ongoing Process

Although most of the visioning sessions I organize last two to three hours, it is really an ongoing process with no stopping and starting point. My clients often ask how many people they should invite to their visioning sessions. I suggest a group of eight to ten people—large enough to get differing views yet small enough to be intimate.

I prefer visioning sessions to be in a low-tech/high-touch environment. Of course, you can record the session either via audio or video, but be sure to get everyone's permission in advance and be aware that the higher tech it is, the less interactive it might be. There is something very visceral and personal about holding a pencil and paper in your hands versus speaking into a microphone or a video camera.

Sharing Visions

During my interview with Reverend Cynthia, she told me the story of a nomadic tribe that travels throughout the day and then meets in a circle every evening. During these meetings each member shares his or her visions. This tribe believes that everyone has a piece of the puzzle. This is a profound concept, especially given our modern world in which we are often isolated from our families of origin and sometimes even colleagues at work, if we telecommute. The power of community and input from others is clearly important and too often lacking in many of our lives.

Passport to Possibility

My personalized variation on the visioning session—an exercise that you can do on your own at home—helps people discover where they are now. Just like those signs in shopping centers that read You Are Here, before you plot your path to your vision, this simple system will enable you to zero in on where you are in your life and what's important to you right now. It's an eye-opening pre-board exercise.

- **Gather up several different kinds of magazines:** If you're into motorcycles, pick up a sailing publication; if you're a city person, pick up *Country Living*. Make sure these are not the usual publications that you read. Pick at least three different magazines, but no more than five.

- **Page through the magazines:** Look through them page by page from beginning to end, just glancing at each page. Don't read any of the stories, not even the captions. Just look at the pictures.

- **Now go back and start with the first magazine you paged through:** Pull out two or three pictures of anything that appeals to you—anything—a travel ad showing a beach, a fashion layout picturing eveningwear, a picture of a flock of birds flying in formation. Continue with the remaining magazines. You should pull out at least eight to ten pictures. Then, put the magazines away.

- **Lay out the pictures:** Place three or four images in a row, not unlike you might display playing cards if you were setting up a solitaire game.

- **Look at the pictures:** Stand up and walk around the table, glancing at the pictures from right to left, upside down, and back to facing them again.

- **Shuffle the pictures:** Do this until you get a sense of how they "fit together"—it's a gut thing. Maybe something about the colors, the design, or the actual content of the images seems to go into a certain sequence.

- **Grab a pencil and pad of paper:** Write down "possible" life opportunities or "destinations."

Here are some hints to help interpret these "defining images":

- **Is there any obvious link?** All outdoor scenes such as beaches, mountains, and airplanes may mean that you want to go on vacation before you manifest your vision; or maybe travel and tourism are part of your dream come true.

- **Look at the POV (point of view):** Are the people (if any) active or static in the images? What does that signify about your own life? Are you the driver or the passenger on your current journey? Which would you like to be? Is it time to just relax or is there a quantum leap ahead?

- **What in the pictures is different from your current way of life?** Are there lots of faces of children, yet you are childless? Or is there one person leading a group, when you are usually in the student role? Consider which role appeals to you most now—newbie or expert.

- **Is there a quality of life sparked by the pictures?** Is it peacefulness, fun, or adventure? Write down some key words.

Still stumped? Shuffle the pictures around again and role-play with yourself. Stand up and advise the you who was sitting in the chair a minute ago. What is your interpretation of the images for him or her? This part of the exercise may make more sense if you are speaking into a cell phone camera or a video camera. Sharing your own inner wisdom is an amazing experience if you've never done it before. Summarize the experience by writing or recording a paragraph or two of "advice" to yourself.

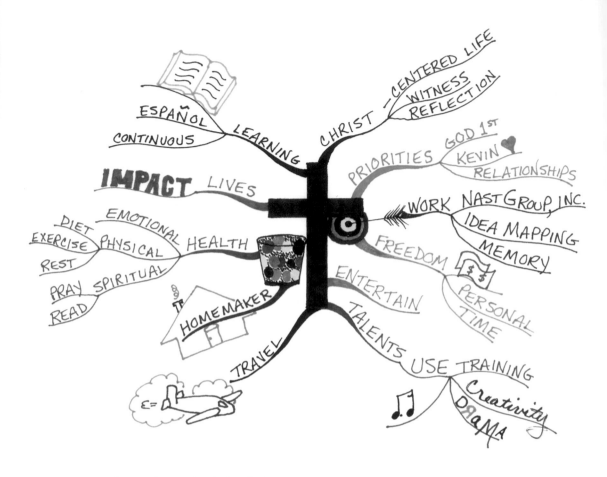

One of my clients had the following insight after completing the exercise:

"It showed me that I'm too into my stuff. I picked out pictures of expensive glassware and a watch decorated in diamonds but when I really looked at the images, I realized I wanted more self-esteem and in the past I've turned to acquiring possessions. What I really want now is inner peace and a sense of who I can be—like the rest of the pictures that showed butterflies nestled into a flower bed and a sunrise that gave me a sense that I have only just begun, even though I'm fifty years old."

And suddenly happiness
of being
what I know for sure
entered me.
Kindness
Being in Balance

(opposite) *This is Jamie Nast's personal mission. Her basic idea map has not changed since 1998. The central images in this idea map represent her desire to live a Christ-centered life and to have clearly defined goals. The image of the bucket of rocks surrounded by pebbles represents an activity used in the Stephen Covey workshops. It reminds her to keep focus on people.*

(top) *A sense of peacefulness and acceptance of self is revealed in Katy Taylor's handmade vision board.*

YOUR PERSONAL VISION STATEMENT

One picture may be worth a thousand words, but in this chapter you will discover that the value of having a personal vision statement—one word or phrase that you craft to visualize your best possible future—is priceless. That's why I recommend you take time to draft your personal vision statement prior to creating your vision board.

Done right, all of the inspirational visioning experiences described in chapter one will spark certain words or phrases and defining images that reflect the future that awaits. From that list you may be "drawn" to a particular word. Later in this chapter you'll see how a motto or song may just hit you and become a source of inspiration.

For an overview of this process and to see how powerful the system can be, check out the featured example of how the Shroyer family combined their motto and vision statement into one compelling power word: freedom. Today they are living their vision come true.

Mary Anne Erickson, Eyes Wide Open

Life loves to be taken by the lapels and told, "I am with you kid, Let's go."

—Maya Angelou

CASE STUDY:

Picking up anchor and setting sail: the Shroyers live their vision of freedom.

Who hasn't dreamed of changing their course in life? Maybe even sailing off into the sunset away from the hustle and bustle of everyday frustrations? For most people the vision is just a romantic idea you only see in movies or read about in books.

For Keith and Susan Shroyer, from Seattle, it took just one word "freedom" to change their lives and power their shared dream come true. "Freedom" serves as their guiding vision statement and motto and mantra all rolled into one. They are a living example of how a strong defining image can spur you to set off on your own journey to an extraordinary life.

In 2007, Susan and the Shroyers' two children, then ages nine and eleven, were waiting for Keith to come home from his job as a mechanical engineer. It was work he had grown to hate. As he tells it in his own words:

> *"I was trapped in a dead-end job with no apparent way out. Either my world was going to break or I was. The lie of the wage-slave paradigm was becoming more evident every day. 'Work for 40 years, go into debt and die poor' was no longer going to work for me. I wanted an up and out plan! Yet, no one was getting this in my family."*

Shroyer created what he now calls his "vision wall"—a life-size, ten-by-twelve-foot "vision board." He selected one well-chosen power word that became not only a motto and mantra but also a vision statement and a background for their gigantic vision board. He took a can of spray paint and literally spelled out "freedom" on the living room wall, in bright red paint with letters more than five feet high. Looking back on that day and his family's reaction he says, "I'm sure they all thought I was crazy at the time."

As he explains, "In retrospect, my wage-slave paradigm was an illusion. Freedom is now my truth. If you make "freedom" your defining thought and send this out to the universe, you get "freedom." In *The Secret* they say, "your job is the 'What,' the Universe tells you 'How.'"

The right power word—in this case "Freedom"—can serve as a vision statement, motto, and even background for an inspiring vision wall, as shown by the Shroyer family who share a dramatic story of change.

After the dramatic moment was over and the gigantic "freedom" was starkly contrasting against their white wall, Keith called a family meeting explaining his feelings of frustration and need for freedom in his life. This was a defining moment in all their lives. He remembers thinking, What would they do next? What was their vision for the future?

Boating was their favorite thing in the world to do, and their vehicle of freedom. For the Shroyers, the defining image was a picture of a forty-foot schooner. Keith recalls, "I tore that picture out of a sailing magazine and I stared at it so much that soon I thought I was on the boat."

Today the Shroyers are living their vision. They sold their house and with the proceeds of that and their newfound vocation of trading stocks online they bought another sailboat and were ready to live out their vision. "Our lives today have us all very free," explains Keith. "We live on sailboats. One is in Kemah, Texas, for winter sun and fun and one in Anacortes, Washington, for summer sun and fun. We migrate with the seasons. I home school our two kids and earn money with Internet stock trading when we need some. Right now we have several years of funds in our money pool and zero debt."

The Shroyers: Living Their Vision

Here's how the Shroyers empowered themselves to live out their vision.

Vision Statement: A powerful word—"freedom"—that also serves as their ongoing mantra and motto.

Vision Board: Literally spray painted on the wall of their house in Seattle. It was embellished with key words, goals, and a wish list for their future. Shroyer enlisted his wife and children to participate in his vision.

Defining Image: A picture of a forty-foot sailboat that Shroyer tore from a magazine.

Visioning: For the Shroyer family the real visioning began after Keith spray painted the wall. Sometimes a dramatic action precedes the more formal visioning process.

Here's how they lived out the law of attraction GRABS formula:

Gratitude: The Shroyers say their gratitudes daily at sunrise and sunset when they look out at the world completely content because they are living their vision.

Release and Receive: They were willing to release their old lives and much of their material possessions to make the transition from large home to forty-foot sailboat possible. Even before Keith came home that night and spray painted "freedom" on the wall, he was ready to receive an answer that would set himself and his family off on inspired action that would enable them to live an extraordinary life.

Ask and Acknowledge: Once Keith sat his family down for a meeting, ideas and visions from all of the family members began to flow; they were asking for what they wanted. It was their responsibility to come up with the "what was next" and to acknowledge that a higher power would figure out the "how of making it happen."

Be and Believe: During this process, they focused on being their authentic selves. As the Shroyers began to vision life on a sailboat their belief became even more real. As Keith stared at their defining image of a forty-foot schooner, he could feel himself setting sail. The Shroyers shored up their belief with weekly phone coaching with Bob Proctor and later Keith and Susan enrolled in Mark Victor Hansen's Millionaires course to discover a new way of making income so that Keith could finally quit his job as a mechanical engineer.

and

Share: Today the Shroyers share their story and their vision with everyone they meet. They are going to blog about their summer adventure sailing along the coast and their new lives. Not surprisingly along the way they faced opposition and criticism from friends and family who thought they were crazy to uproot from Seattle and leave steady work. Today some of those same naysayers want to do the same thing.

How This Worked for the Shroyers

What made this vision possible for the Shroyers was a combination of a strong vision, and the constant reminder and encouragement their vision wall provided. Goals and key words added to the life-size vision board in addition to some powerful coaching from some of the top wisdom leaders and inspired action and advice from me—I encouraged them to set sail now not at some vague time in the future—helped. Every day, morning and night, they reinforce their vision and their belief in their choice by saying their gratitudes, acknowledging their good fortune and bravery, and continuing their spiritual lessons by listening to their favorite inspirational teachers.

As can be seen from their story, living the vision is an ongoing process not a one-time unhooking of the anchor to the past. Keeping the vision fresh and navigating day-to-day challenges is a process even when you're sailing on a forty-foot schooner.

(right) *Life is a feast and you'll want to share your bounty with mentors, partners, supporters, and new fans along the way like Jennifer Lee of Artizen Coaching.* (far right) *Post visual cues like Lee's* Womanifesto *to keep power words and your vision statement top of mind—and follow her lead and take time to chronicle how your life vision is unfolding in your own online blog.*

The Art and Science of Crafting Your Vision

Crafting a vision statement or picking the key words that match your core values is not just a matter of making a list and checking it twice. There is an art and a science to creating your guiding vision statement and later your vision board. It's not an abracadabra potion or magic spell you say and then suddenly you begin living your vision.

Is it any wonder that magical thinking sets in after people quickly paste up their vision boards without taking time to create a vision statement or adopt a life motto to provide momentum to their vision. All too often when I look at blogs online or when people say to me that visioning doesn't work for them or that they tried a vision board and nothing happened I realize that their vision statement didn't come from their heart nor was it soul-inspired.

It was just another to-do on their chores list—like fixing the faucet—and when they were done they didn't acknowledge it or the steps they'd made toward their goals. The joy went down the drain.

Check online and you'll find most guides for creating a vision board simply say to cut out pictures from a magazine, glue them to a poster board, and add a few words or phrases. Most people spend more time cooking a nice dinner than they do creating a vision board. Remember this process is all about transforming your life, so it will take some work. But you're worth it.

Begin by using some of the key information revealed during your visioning process in the first stage of crafting your personal vision statement.

Gather Your Information

- ✦ **Check visioning notes:** Reread your notes from the visioning activities and highlight them with a highlighter or transfer them from writing or audio or video to a large whiteboard.

- ✦ **Find visuals:** Think about any images that were mentioned or kept "coming up" in the visioning process; for example, in a visioning session I had for this book, several images were mentioned and I received several more: visions of a woman in a purple robe, a vision of me speaking to large audiences, me traveling around the world. So I created some visuals for those to use later on a vision board.

- ✦ **Look at role models:** During my visioning session someone mentioned Joan of Arc, which at first made me shiver a bit, but then I realized that I had made many vital decisions in my life at age fourteen. So perhaps what the Joan of Arc reference was supposed to do was to remind me to become fourteen again and recapture that youthful experience in visioning my life.

Turn the Inside Out

To really move forward in the vision statement creation process, you'll want to supplement your visioning experience notes and images with:

✦ Your "You-powered Youniverse" activity results (page 33).

✦ The motto that you select or craft in the "Motto Mojo" section, page 35, and the revised motto that truly reflects your dreams come true.

✦ Your wish lists—everyone has some wish lists around somewhere— in the back of a diary, hidden in your lingerie drawer, scrawled on an old address book, or as an addendum to your to-do list in your online calendar. Be sure to distinguish from your day-to-day chore list and the real heartfelt wishes or what they called the bucket list in the movie of the same name.

- ✦ Make a list of the top ten things you are thankful for in your life (see "Gratitude" activity, page 55, for ideas).

- ✦ Select an affirmation that empowers you in the creation of your vision statement, such as:

  My vision statement is revealed effortlessly and empowers me to live not only my best possible life but to contribute significantly to the world.

- ✦ Get inspired by other people's vision statements.

(left) The appeal of wishing upon a star is universal; these wish cards were left at Asian temples and photographed by Amy Ho. Turning wishes into reality is one reason to create a vision statement. (below) Jessica Smith's wish list, depicted on her board, is very specific and heartfelt.

Vision Statement Checklist

Ask these questions of your vision statement:

✦ Is it a vivid, idealized description of the outcome that you want and the future you're creating? In my experience, an effective vision statement is memorable and empowered by passion and positive emotion. If yours is not powerful—if it doesn't truly inspire you—then craft another!

✦ Is it too long? While some people might promote the merits of a lengthy vision statement—a few paragraphs or even a page or so—I suggest you edit it so that it is ten words or less. Later in this chapter you'll see how focusing on just one strong word may form an empowering vision.

✦ Does your vision statement need more punch? If you're still feeling that your vision statement is lacking power, you may need more inspiration. Consider these options for adding some zest to your vision statement:

  • One or two empowering words, such as "Let's Roll!"

  • A memorable phrase that you craft yourself (for example, Muhammad Ali's motto, Float Like a Butterfly, Sting Like a Bee).

  • Use a variation of a popular song or movie title ("I Can See Clearly Now" from the Johnny Nash song).

  • A new twist on an age-old motto or favorite quotation (the famous Jem'Hadar characters on Star Trek shout, "Victory is life!").

  • A mash-up or juxtaposition of an advertising slogan ("I am all I can be," a variation of the U.S. Army slogan Be All You Can Be!).

  • A spin off from a favorite song. One of my own vision statements is a special spin on a favorite inspirational song from Man of La Mancha, Live the Possible Dream, a variation of "Dream the Impossible Dream!"

✦ Is it highly personal—you get it and are reminded of it daily, maybe hourly by something you do in real life? For example, opening doors is a vision statement that I refer to especially when I feel like I'm starting a new project and feel like a "stranger in a strange land." I tell myself, "Open the door for others but walk through first."

Often people ask how I came up with that. When I was in high school I came up with a great idea to turn the school paper into a daily versus a weekly. When the advisor asked for nominations for the new editor, I naively thought my friends would toss my name into the ring. They didn't. That was when I decided I better lead the parade I was organizing. Sure I've taken some arrows in my back now and then, but as a scout and pioneer I reap many rewards too.

Your vision statement may come from a personal experience—a childhood dream or from a play or song that has stayed with you over the years. It may be a variation of a favorite quote or it may just be revealed to you by your higher power or creative consciousness one day. If you're already the spiritual type you may easily see how the well of opportunity can bubble forth and the right words or phrases are "channeled to you."

Need some inspiration? Check out the personal vision statements of famous people that are featured in this book and others that may be personal role models.

Never doubt that a small group of thoughtful, committed people can change the world. Indeed it is the only thing that ever has.

—Margaret Mead

What you do speaks so loudly that I cannot hear what you say.

—Ralph Waldo Emerson

Where to Find Inspiration for Your Vision Statement

Ideas can be found in many places and from many sources. Here are a few:

- ✦ A variation of a favorite quote

- ✦ A favorite children's book such as *The Little Engine That Could*

- ✦ A TV show or movie trailer

- ✦ A mural or wall graffiti

- ✦ From "Motto Mojo" *(see page 35)*

- ✦ Revisiting your top values *(see "Values" activity, page 37)*

- ✦ Selecting a "Defining Image" *(see page 42)*

- ✦ Start with a wish list first and then form a "summary wish" that you can reword into a vision statement that inspires you to not just wish but also win.

Vision Statement vs. Mission Statement

To clarify the purpose of a vision statement, I often explain to my clients that it is like a GPS navigation system now featured in most new cars: it enables you to map out alternate routes to your destination. Don't confuse your personal vision statements with old-fashioned and stuffy corporate mission statements. Getting you on the route to inspired action is crucial to realizing the fruits of the law of attraction.

Back in the 1980s and early 1990s corporate mission statements were all the rage. Usually costly consultants were hired to draft a corporate mission and then lead an offsite retreat where ivory tower executives got middle managers to adopt the pledge of new buzzwords. The mission statement filtered from the top down and gave way to departmental mission slogans and team songs; you were rewarded for your buy-in of the corporate mission. Gradually, mission statements took on the form of corporate slogans.

A decade or so ago visioning would have seemed very "new age" or "touchy-feely" in the corporate world. So the personal vision statement gained power from the grassroots up—by people who wanted to realize their own personal power as innovators or entrepreneurs or, yes, visionaries.

A great vision statement can be used to enhance any part of your life. Many people craft a vision statement for such areas as family, health, wealth (abundance), and cause-related projects. You may want to craft a different vision statement for each major event in your life such as a birthday, an anniversary, starting a new job, and for major goals such as buying a dream house, changing careers, or launching your own business.

Connect with You First: You-Power!

Even before you begin to craft your vision statement or adopt some mottoes and reinforce them with affirmations, you can get started. You can reconnect to that center you found in the visioning exercise anytime you want and it's wise to daily take a well-deserved time-out when you get hungry, angry, lonely, or tired and revitalize through meditation or other fun and play activities and positive people that reconnect you with the one-ness of it all—the "Youniverse."

You-Powered Youniverse

At the back of this book or on a separate sheet of paper, write down the statements that are true for you today.

- I am connected to a supportive group of positive and loving friends.

- I nurture and value my family of choice by keeping in touch daily or weekly via phone or email. ("Family" members could include friends and colleagues—whoever you rely on for support.)

- I am active in online social networking such as MySpace.com or Facebook.com, or business systems such as LinkedIn.com.

- I value people more than process or products while I'm working.

- I rekindle my childlike sense of wonder daily by taking time to play and to not just smell but plant roses (or whatever other hobby you enjoy).

- I feel a strong connection to most of the people that I meet and live near or with.

- I have people I can call at 3 a.m. when the going gets rough or when I need to get going.

- I have a motto that motivates me forward when I come to a crack in the road.

- I have taken a vacation or a sabbatical from work in the past year.

- I balance work and leisure.

- I have been actively involved in some kind of public service or community outreach work in the past year.

- I know what my life's mission is and the Youniverse has confirmed I'm on track in the past month.

Count the number of statements that you wrote down.

10 to 12 statements: Your You-power is healthy and vibrant. You are ready to move on to create your life vision or to update your personal vision.

7 to 9 statements: Your You-power is dwindling. You may want to consider taking a station break (see page 36) or at least a well-deserved mental health day to rekindle your natural resources.

6 or fewer: You are tired. You need to take a station break, clear your calendar of all that you can, cash in those vacation days due, and begin to repair the cracks in your Youniverse. This will help prepare you to move forward.

The challenge with "You-power" in real life is that you also have the power to create the negative too—to listen to those random thoughts in your head and think they are true. Instead you need to strip away that false data. Otherwise you may stop your future in its path to fruition.

Timing Is Everything

Though timing is everything, many of my clients want to force their way into the next door—kick it down or take a magic potion that will give them comic-book powers to zap right through the wall they've hit. If you are currently in the midst of a major financial or personal crisis— if your house is in jeopardy of being repossessed or your child is just diagnosed with a serious illness—now may not be the time to ponder the future of your whole life. You may want to craft a vision statement that gets you through this day that enables you to reframe your mind and your life.

But don't postpone the process too long! Otherwise it's inevitable that "inter-fearence" will set in and you will freeze in place. You tell yourself and others it will be different in the summer when the kids are out of school or after you take that trip to Disney World or when your husband graduates from law school or that you will create a vision statement together with your new partner.

Our inter-fearence diverts our own power and we forget to take a station break for our own self-identification and lose our ability to live our lives with energy on a high frequency. Static sets in, like when cable goes out and we just see fuzzy snow. We've lost the signal, even though the picture is not gone!

Motto Mojo

Still not inspired enough to craft a powerful vision statement? Add a little "motto mojo" to the mix and it may make it easier. Try "redrafting" or "mashing up" (adding a little bit of this and a lot of that) to a popular motto, ad slogan, or even an historic quotation.

One of the first questions I ask my new clients is what motto they were raised with—you know, a favorite saying of family members. Your parents may have had a different one or maybe you adopted a motto or saying of an older brother or grandparent who was influential. My mom's was "The Sun Will Come Out Tomorrow" and my dad's was "Your Day Will Come." Is it any wonder I spent the first part of my life yearning to live in the future and not appreciating the present?

Think about and write down the following:

◆ What was your family's motto?

◆ Did you have your own personal slogan or mantra that kept you motivated when you were a child? If so, what was it?

Rethinking Your Motto

Occasionally a client will get into a rut and find himself complaining that "life is the pits." This becomes that person's motto. How can you give a more positive spin on a negative motto or mantra? Change "Life is the pits" to "Life is just a bowl of cherries," or instead of always saying, "I'm going nuts," adopt an oldie but goodie like "I'm cool as a cucumber."

Sure it may sound zany, even corny, but try it. Besides you don't have to share this exercise with anyone else!

Are You Being Authentic to Your Own Values?

Values are like the indicators on a compass—they help you find your way north, south, east, and west—and they work under the most dire circumstances. Even in a storm of challenge you can refer to your values as indicators of what's important to you and use them as navigators for your next steps. See if the vision statement you're crafting is on target and really reflects the authentic you or is just mirroring back what you think your peers would like to hear you say about your future.

Values and Vision Statements

You can use your values to create your vision statement or get back on course if you're lost along the way.

Lets say that your top three values are 1) freedom 2) excitement 3) environment. If your current job is working on the assembly line at a factory that makes disposable plastic cups you may be in conflict with your values. What to do?

Station Break

This is a time-out or a sabbatical that you take to allow time to self-identify. A station break may be a few days or weeks or even months or a year. It's a play on the station break television programs and radio programs used to make to announce that you were watching a certain channel or listening to a certain station.

Aside from taking the drastic step of quitting, you could begin to come in closer proximity to your values by doing some volunteer work with a local organization—or suggest that the R&D department in your company try to create a better cup that is biodegradable. What about inspiring your company to donate money to a charity of its choice to support clean water for every pack of disposable cups that are sold? There are lots of options.

But what is your bigger picture? Now you're ready to begin to reclaim your destiny. Go ahead and renumber your values or shuffle them around—it's your life!

What Do You Value?

Your vision statement is driven by your strongest personal values. What do you value? What's important to you?

At the back of this book or on a separate sheet of paper, list your top ten values.

Having trouble? Frame it with the phrase I value_____ and then insert the words.

If you're still having trouble, go to your favorite search engine and hit the tab labeled "images." Type in the search word "values" and see what comes up. Pictures may be more powerful than words.

Not sure which value is most important to you? Try this: place these values that are common quests for many of us in order from most to least important.

acknowledgment	freedom	power	security
environment	friends	recognition	spirituality
excitement	honesty	reputation	
family	money	respect	

Disagree with these or feel they are not values? Now you're beginning to feel these from your gut. Begin the list now. If you can't come up with ten, then list five—but do this fast.

Vision Statement Tips and Tricks

Tips As You Go

Often clients have challenges finding time to create their vision statements, and sometimes they wonder if they are on the right track. Here are some additional tips that may empower you to move forward:

✦ **Edit your statement:** Can't get it down to 10 words or less? Start by summarizing your vision in one to four sentences max.

+ **Sort out the key words first.** It's easier to start with some key words. Use your values (see Values activity, page 37).

+ **Ignore "stuff":** Focus on the big picture of your life not the stuff (cars, houses, trips, and new clothes); sort the value of them when you're ready to create your vision board.

+ **Turn it over:** Let go and let God or your creative source guide you.

+ **Think why, not what or how:** The why is important—think your destiny and your legacy—don't worry about the *what* or the *how* right now.

+ **Reach inside, experience the future now:** Go ahead and be emotional, and refer back to some of those words and terms and visuals that evolved from your visioning exercise. How do you feel now that you have achieved those things?

+ **Think in the future but act in the present:** This is the past tense in advance. As a journalist I've learned to past tense in advance. Play your story out in your mind as if it is already happening.

Two Secrets to Vision Statements Revealed

+ **Suspend disbelief:** Remember that anything and everything is possible. You already learned this valuable technique during your visioning exercises or hopefully even before you began those activities. But sometimes you have to remind yourself. Suspend disbelief just as you do when you see a movie. Imagine yourself snuggled into a comfy chair about to see the story of your life on the big screen.

+ **Make sure it stands the test of time:** Think ballpark vs. small details. Just because you're thinking ballpark, you don't have to think the game of life is like baseball or football. Life is more random than linear.

Four No-Sweat Ways to Your Personal Vision Statement

✦ **Write it on the back of a napkin:** This is great to do at restaurants or on a long plane trip. That's one way to keep it short and sweet.

✦ **Scrawl it on a notebook:** One sentence of ten words or less can form a highly personal vision statement. A vision statement can be playful and fun. You can handwrite variations of it at a coffee shop or in an airport if you don't want to hole up in an office to create your vision statement.

✦ **Use sticky notes:** Those colorful little self-adhesive notes make great placeholders for your vision statement. Try putting just one word on each one and organizing them on a door or a bulletin board or even your desk. You can also use them to create a "wish list." See the "Wishboard" image (page 40, bottom) that was created for the Saratoga "First Night" (New Year's Eve/Day Celebration) in Saratoga, New York, where sticky notes were placed on a large billboard. The "To Do!" guerilla artwork project in Brooklyn, New York, created by the group "Illegal Artists," encouraged pedestrians to add their own "To Do!" to a display on the side of a building that featured a total of 5,600 sticky flags.

✦ **Go graffiti:** On the boardwalk in Venice, California, there is a Graffiti Wall where you can spray paint your vision statement and take a picture of it. Within ten minutes someone will have painted over your creation. Other cities offer legal areas for graffiti—or consider a chalk design that you snap digital pictures of after you're done. You can also try the Digital Graffiti collaborative experience provided on this book's Web site by a design firm called The Broth. Try using just words and then include some kind of defining image if you wish. Be sure to save your design to your own laptop or desktop or to take a scan or screen grab of it before it disappears. Start by "painting on" some key words or just one powerful word such as "Freedom" like the Shroyer family did (pages 22–25).

(right) There are many uses for sticky flags. Here, they drive the vision home by highlighting power words. ("Yes!" by Akum Norder)

(bottom) Wishes do come true. First Night in Saratoga Springs, NY, is a family-oriented, nonalcoholic celebration of the arts organized by the community and the YMCA. Attendees express their visions for the future with sticky notes on the Wish Board sponsored in the center of town by GE. First Night celebrations are held annually on New Year's Eve in 111 cities around the world.

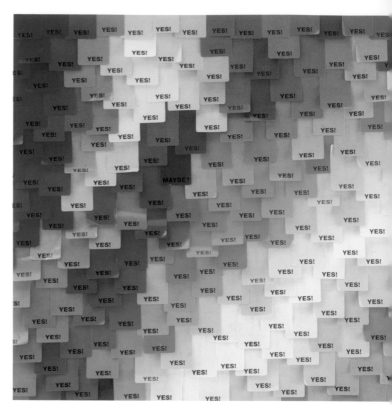

Cautions During Creation

◆ **Be prepared for randomness:** Embrace it—that's what makes life exciting. There's no reason that you have to be cautious when creating your vision statement.

◆ **Beware of including dates:** Don't fence yourself in by including this afternoon or tonight or tomorrow or at least a taste of it.

◆ **Don't let money or lack of it stop you—you don't have to be rich to live your vision:** You could be sampling your vision every day no matter how much money you have in your checking or whether you're still in school. Prosperity comes in many ways, and the universal bank is always delivering which is why you have to be ready to receive.

How To Use Your Vision Statement

◆ Post it where you can see it.

◆ Check it daily.

◆ Revise it at the start of every season (summer, fall, winter, spring).

◆ Carry a copy of it on a small card in your wallet.

◆ Add it to your vision board.

◆ Create or acquire some visual reminders.

◆ Print it on the back of your business cards.

Sample Defining Images

Heart with Wings: A past client, Judith Parker Harris, creator of the Health Esteem wellness program, chose this symbol as one of her favorite defining images to visualize sharing her inner heart with others.

Happiness Day: This logo was created for International Happiness Day, which occurs on July 10 each year.

Peace Please: This is both a logotype (customized typeface) and a variation on the international peace symbol.

Vision Statement Visuals

Defining Image

In my work I've found that many of my clients come to me and already have in their mind or in print a defining visual image that guides them in their career or personal life. Often it's a common symbol such as a butterfly or a powerful word such as "change" or "victory"; sometimes it's a logotype (visual typeface) of a favorite saying or quotation. What is your defining image? How can you use it to spur you on to create a powerful vision statement?

The Importance of Visual Reminders

You can't carry your vision statement and vision board with you everywhere so that it's a reminder to you. Sure you can post the vision statement or carry a card in your wallet but often you need more to propel you forward to reach your goals and seek adventure in life. That's when visual reminders become valuable.

Here are some ideas of what you can use to create visual reminders that will serve you well throughout your day, whether you're in the office, at home, or traveling.

- ✦ A baseball cap with your defining image on it.

- ✦ Jewelry that includes or hints at your defining image.

- ✦ Buttons and/or pins that you can wear with your defining image on them.

- ✦ A lap quilt that you can use as a throw while reading or watching TV.

- ✦ A ring that you can create or have designed with your symbol on it.

- ✦ An image you can place on your cell phone as wallpaper.

Other possibilities: What about a vision journal or a digital photo that has meaning for you? My defining image is a picture of me in front of the People's Hall in Beijing, China. If I can get there from the projects in Ohio I can do anything!

Your Power Word

As you read in the Shroyer family story, they created one power word "freedom" that served as a vision statement and defining image for their best possible future. You too may find that one special word is the passkey to unlock the portal to the extraordinary life of your dreams. Where does that word come from? How do you find that special phrase? My clients have told me that one word is often just "channeled to them" from a higher power. Others say that they keep hearing the same word over and over on the radio or TV, or see it on the Internet or on billboards.

Sometimes that one word can be a place. Hawaii or Paris or Paradise or Utopia may resonate with you to symbolize the future that awaits. Or, if it's a real city, that place may be a destination along the route that you should take to creating your future. If you can't go there now, then try a virtual visit online or by reading books about the area or about spiritual practices of that area or even its history. As I tell my clients, just keep your antenna up and your notebook ready. The word will be revealed—after all, you already know what it is! Check your visioning session notes; it could be that the word was repeated several times during that experience. Or it could be the opposite of a word that symbolizes something negative in your life today. Make sure the word is powerful and drives you forward.

Armed with your personal motto, your power word or phrases, your favorite quotations, and your streamlined vision statement, you're ready to move on to the creation of your vision board. Don't forget your defining image; you may want to spotlight it on your board. Since my image includes a picture of me, I find that it is an ongoing reminder of not only how far I've come in life but also how far I can reach around the world to live my best possible future.

Mary Anne Erickson

CREATING VISION BOARDS

Vision boards are much more than the sum of their parts—more than just pictures, words, phrases, glitter, and glue. Vision boards are essential tools that

+ focus you on what's really important in your life;

+ clarify your true vision, which may be hidden by all the "stuff" in your life;

+ enhance your inner awareness, because you're expending energy, time, and commitment to focus on your future;

+ assist you in finding the authentic you, not a "put on a happy face" manufactured facade;

+ help you find out what makes you special—what differentiates you from others—by enabling you to visually express what you want in life based on your personal values;

+ move you out of your day-to-day patterns and reframe your own opinions about yourself so they are more positive and optimistic;

+ help you unlock the secret to an extraordinary life by revealing your authentic self—the you that you truly are.

All true artists, whether they know it or not, create from a place of no-mind, from inner stillness.

—Eckhart Tolle

Celebrate creativity when making your vision boards, as Mary Anne Erickson does in I Create.

Begin With Your Vision Statement

Creating your personal vision statement in advance of actually designing your vision board is helpful because it enables you to find and focus on inspiring phrases. You can then take those phrases and edit them down to a handful of "power words"—words that resonate with you and help you to see your vision clearly. The wording of your vision statement itself will be valuable in developing the visual format and assist in the selection of images to use on your board.

As an example, one of my vision statements is to "Open the door for others but walk through first." What would visually represent that vision to me? The first thought is "doors," but if I relax and enjoy the creation exercise, I find that it's not just traditional doors made of wood, stone, or metal—it's new frontiers like those I've delved into in the areas of multimedia and film, as well as visiting new countries.

So it's more the metaphorical "new door"—the untrodden path, the fork in the road—than the literal. These ideas easily inspire my new power words: new frontier, beyond the summit, opportunity, and respect. While writing this chapter, I recalled the quote from Aras Baskauskas, who won the million-dollar prize in *Survivor*, that "doors will open by themselves." No pushing, no pulling, no kicking them down . . . just watching them open as if automatically or responding to my sheer presence.

The Tolle quote at the beginning of the chapter is insightful since it assures us that we can fuel our creative process by seeking inner stillness rather than just frenetic activity. Take time to review your notes from your visioning experience before gathering pictures, sorting images, and defining your power words.

+ Review your visioning experience notes for key words or phrases that strike you as relevant to your vision.

Left Brain, Right Brain

Typical life planning focuses on left-brain methods— logical, sequential, and analytical. Yet it is the power of the right hemisphere of your brain, the more creative aspects—random, intuitive, holistic, and synthesizing—that allow you to move past organized routine and the status quo to better not only your life but also the world.

Do you see yourself soaring with eagles? Beverly Keaton-Smith's visual creation goes beyond the board as "words within words" add a sense of vibrancy to her vision.

✦ Write out a large version of your vision statement or its variations and post it on your desk or the area where you'll be designing your board.

✦ Decide if you want to create an overview or panorama vision board or a vision board for a particular area of your life or future event, such as your wedding, the birth of your child, or a graduation. An overview board is the kind that most of my clients created before discovering through my process and exercises that pasting fifty pictures on one board might not be as effective a visual-motivation tool as it would be to do focused vision boards for specific aspects of their lives.

✦ Flip through the book's later chapters—Relationships, Gratitude, and Wealth and Well-being—to find boards you can use for reference to inspire you if you're stuck. The vision boards in these chapters are divided into even more specific topics; for example, in Relationships, you'll see samples of boards for love, romantic relationships, and family, among others.

Moving Away from Magical Thinking

Vision boards eliminate the biggest pitfall of most motivational methods—magical thinking. Instead of just thinking about the future—hoping and wishing and eventually even obsessing about it—vision boards enable you to literally create the visions of your dreams today. They let you create your future in a much more visceral fashion. They work from the inside out not outside in: you are creating from inspiration not from others' motivations and desires.

Key Vision Board Elements

Most of the vision boards in this book and others you may see likely include the following components:

- **Visuals**: images/snapshots, photographs, and drawings

- **Quotations and Mantras:** favorite sayings, mantras, mottoes, or actual quotes from role models

- **Affirmations:** positive sayings that inspire you to live your best possible life. Form these phrases so that they are in the present tense and always positive: "I am" "I have" versus the more passive "I wish" or "I would like."

- **Power Words:** These are based on the themes that evolve from your visioning experience, such as "freedom" and "abundance." I like to add words that connote excitement, such as "play," "fun," and "vacation" so that I remind myself of the importance of balance in my life.

  - *Sample relationship power words:* attraction, appreciation, communication, closeness, care, loyalty, support, trust

  - *Sample family power words:* quality time, shared values, acknowledgment, health, respect, love, optimism, gratitude, unity, self-reliance

  - *Sample health power words:* vibrant, energetic, active, fit, glowing, calm, strong, healing, relaxed, rejuvenated

  - *Sample gratitude power words:* give, share, thank, welcome, appreciate, acknowledge

If you're creating your vision board from scratch, you'll need to gather the components in advance to ensure that you have all the elements on hand when you start. Some people use digital software packages that provide guidance in the process, including prompts for visuals, quotations and mantras, affirmations, and power words.

(left) *A colorful handmade vision board like this one by Katy Taylor uses text and images to question how she wants to live. Often called an inspiration board, this variation of a vision board is great to turn to as you move into a new house or begin your marriage; it can also serve as a life collage for the upcoming year.*

(below) *This board, by Monica Austin, features many power words and positive images.*

The story behind one vision board:
The Goddess of Destiny

I first met Lisa Osborne at one of my workshops at the National Association of Broadcasters, the trade show for television and radio executives. At that time, she was hosting her own radio show about The Internet called the Information Network. Since then, Osborne has gone on to host and produce several different radio shows and other programming, including her popular online site, www.lisa.fm, where she features experts on topics ranging from careers to enhancing your intuition.

What Osborne's board says: Her board portrays her future as the "Goddess of Destiny," the star of a new television show and syndicated programming portal. Sound improbable? Hardly. Osborne captured a picture from an HGTV episode where she portrayed the modern "Goddess of Destiny" and married her friends during an ultramodern ceremony on a TV episode. (She's an ordained minister.)

Elements: Osborne uses the following to create her board: a picture of herself actually performing the real-life role on an HGTV episode. While she's lucky to have a tape of herself already doing what she wants— something not everyone has—you can simulate the feeling of it. Have a friend take a picture of you driving a Ferrari or place a picture of yourself on the top of an image of Mt. Everest. The background to Osborne's board is a photograph of where her home will be in Malibu. Note the "will be," since it is still a vision, but you need to be positive. The picture of a one-million-dollar bill represents the prosperity the show will bring. The numeral "1" symbolizes being the number one show in the nation. "Passionate" and "Provocative" stand for the reviews her show will get; and the ace of spades stands for the ancient "cards of destiny" system that she is revitalizing—blending astrology and numerology with the deck of cards, to help people discover their destinies.

Radio talk-show host Lisa Osborne creates a muted-tone vision that's powerful because of a handful of well-chosen and personalized images and symbols.

Theme: Osborne's theme for her vision board is definitely "the future" but also focuses on work, lifestyle, and a new option for manifesting prosperity, which she portrays visually. For Osborne, this highly visual vision board is very powerful. Another option would be to actually print the words "work," "lifestyle," and "prosperity" on the board, and to add a favorite quote and an affirmation.

Every Vision Board Is Unique

Each vision board is different. Every artist has his or her own view of life, and when creating your vision board it is crucial to express your own style. Why personalize your board? The more you custom-tailor your board to your own interests and add your favorite quotations and power words, the more likely that you will find that it attracts and keeps your attention.

First-time vision-board makers often start with what they think they should have. But what's most important is being truly honest with yourself. Maybe you don't really want a serious boyfriend but just a lover or a movie companion. It's easy to kid yourself by thinking you want what the world says you're supposed to have, but chances are you've tried it that way before and it didn't make you happy. Being true to you is the answer.

Handmade vs. Digital Vision Boards

You'll see handmade vision boards—drawn, collaged, and so on—throughout the book. People who are creating vision boards for the first time may want to actually create theirs totally from scratch, using pictures cut out from magazines, snapshot duplicates from albums, and photographs of places where they want to live or work in the future. Make a large printout or get a posterboard that you can hang on a wall. Later, you can scan the vision board and use it as a screensaver or wallpaper for your cell phone, but the power of the large poster style is invaluable!

I like using a combination of methods to create my own vision boards. A handmade board is an adventure and allows for the ultimate in personalization.

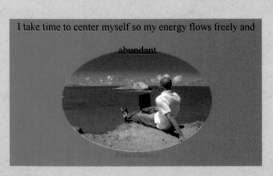

I take time to center myself so my energy flows freely and abundant

You can easily update it by adding a new picture or a special curio. A software-created board is often much quicker to design and can be used as a screensaver or wallpaper for your computer or even your big LCD screen in the living area. So each option has value. High-tech methods allow you to scan your hand-created board and post it both on your home and office walls.

(opposite) *His digital board serves as a reminder of a peaceful place for Cornelis Boertjens.*

(left) *This vision board by Edward Mills demonstrates that you can just tear out pictures and arrange them geometrically or randomly. Big bold type, borders, die-cuts, family photos, and nature scenes complement your personal vision so that you can see tomorrow today!*

> *Be as authentic to the real you as you can using the new knowledge and insight you discover in your visioning experience, during the creation of your vision statement, and during the vision board creation itself.*

(left) *"Freedom" is one of the most popular personal themes that evolves during the visioning process. Personalizing your vision board to reflect your own point of view of what freedom means, like Bethann Shannon did here, is one of the easiest methods to let the "authentic you" out of the closet of your mind. Shannon is a multimedia artist, workshop leader, and peace activist. Her art, including her work based on Mexican artist Frida Kahlo, can be viewed online.*

Reframe Your Thoughts

It's all too easy to get hung up on family, peer, or society labels: you're too fat, you're too old, you're too poor. Instead, reframe your own view of yourself using your new vision statement, power words, and the visuals on your board to enable you to see the good in your life; for example, I am healthy, I am happy to be single again, I enjoy more time with my family and friends, I am wise, I am savvy, I am street-smart.

For many people, just the creation changes their views of the future. For you, it can be an ongoing source of inspiration and affirmation that you can be living your best possible future now.

Until vision boards, the myriad personal development techniques espoused for changing our lives have been only mental and verbal, bypassing the visual. You read and listen to books and tapes and watch videos but you really don't see the vision! Vision boards are a way to physically see the future.

Authenticity requires self-knowledge. Your vision board should reflect your point of view, your values, and your personality style. Your vision board should express your courage to live life based on your inner being and beliefs rather than the demands of your family, society, or peer pressure. Your vision board reflects the best possible you. You can create abundance even if your family of origin had a poverty mentality.

At first glance, some of the boards in this book may appear rather generic, but they become anything but ordinary once you read the explanations about how they empower change. Others are truly works of art. We are all artists at heart, as we create the most precious thing—life—every day. Your vision is your own—it's special and a gift. Vision boards are the most visceral and visual route to "picture your future," who you are, and to experience your destiny today.

"Everything that's coming into your life you are attracting into your life. And it's attracted by virtue of the images you're holding in your mind. It's what you're thinking. Whatever is going on in your mind you are attracting to you."

—**Bob Proctor**

Create From the Inside Out:
Pre-Board Groundwork

As seen in the first two chapters of this book, I've added my own spin
to the traditional "Ask, Believe, and Receive" formula for practicing the law of
attraction, where you attract all aspects of your best possible life to you. One
of the most important steps to creating your vision board is GRABS. It gets you
in the right mind-set for figuring out what goals and experiences are most
important to you—an essential step before creating your boards. Here's how
GRABS works with this process:

G = Gratitude

Before you start the vision board creation process, be sure to say thanks for
the good things and people in your life.

R=Release and Receive

Be ready to release the old and receive the very best possible life now. You can
do this by reaching out to some of your friends from the past, rereading old
holiday cards, and looking at school yearbooks. Refresh yourself with the great

Be Grateful *Activity*

**At the back of this book, or on a separate sheet of paper, write the
following, or you can just think about them.**

I am thankful for _____

I am grateful that _____

I appreciate my _____

Thanks for _____ yesterday.

Capture your best memories in a tribute vision board to salute the greatest moments in your life and many more to come. Here Theda Sandiford's images create an inviting collage that depicts her gratitude.

Best Memories

My top five best memories (or achievements) or successes, or what I'm most proud of, are

1._____

2._____

3._____

4._____

5._____

parts of your life. Count your blessings and focus on good memories. It's likely that the people from your past, from college or even grade school, the old neighborhood, or colleagues from your first job will be valuable in supporting your new journey. These relationships are like fine wine and can be even sweeter than they were before. There's something so validating about talking to a college roommate years later and listening to her or him remind you how far you've come in life. New people in your life are also important. They don't know the you of the past and what others consider your faults or your failings. They are often even more open about who you can be and your new visions of opportunity.

Keep in mind: your memories, achievements, or successes don't have to be monetary or even defined as "success" by the rest of the world. Base them on those experiences that fulfill your personal values, bolster your sense of self, and put you in the flow of your best possible you. Be sure to omit any negative comments that come to mind as you list your best memories. This will put you in the best possible mind-set to receive all of the new ideas about yourself that will propel you forward.

Miracles

One of the first questions I ask my clients is, "Have you experienced a miracle in your life?" Nine times out of ten when people answer the question they discover not only one but many miracles and in that process begin to see their own power of co-creation. Think about it: what are the miracles in your life?

Totally stuck on this one? To provide an example, here are mine: 1) Going to New York at age nineteen to live out my teenage dream of working on a major magazine. 2) Getting into USC film school in less than 3 hours (really!). 3) Getting married. 4) Creating a mini soap-box derby car with a young boy and sharing his smile as he brought home the first-place trophy for best in his class. 5) Co-producing the "day-in-the-life of Paris" virtual experience live online back in 1996.

A = Ask and Acknowledge

After acknowledging yourself and those who have helped you, it's time to ask for insight in selecting and listing your best possible goals for your life from this moment on—not in the future but right now. Can't find the right picture, not sure of how to show the image of a great relationship, wondering if that quote is too old school? Ask and feel what your heart tells you, go further into yourself, and let your soul and inner spirit grab at the correct choice for you. Look at the pictures of boards on similar topics or experiences in this book. What did some of the other artists use to depict success, income streams, or health? If you have access to a computer and can go online, go to one of the search engines and click on images and enter a word or similar words, such as wealth, prosperity, and abundance, and see what pictures come up. Now use those images to spark your search in magazines or other media for your own defining image—the one that will attract you to what you envision.

B = Be and Believe

Bold Defining Images Only

In this style (see image opposite) only images are used and collaged together. Images might include larger-than-life flowers combined with a skyline and a theatrical representation of an artist in white geisha makeup, which symbolizes envisioning a world of opportunity and travel as a stage designer. For another artist, the same images could be rearranged to symbolize adding drama to a humdrum life.

Throughout the process, be your authentic self, and understand that the most important step toward belief in yourself, the universe, and your creative source or higher power may be suspending disbelief. Just as when you walk into a movie theatre, you don't have to believe that the movie is true or even believable, you just suspend your disbelief and trust that Hollywood can make Tinker Bell fly. Believe that you are entitled to your best possible life and a destiny free from struggle. Believe that no matter what happened before, from this moment on, you deserve the best. Inspirational leader Mary Manin Morrissey, who heads LifeSoulutions Inc. and was in *The Moses Code*, compares creating new belief systems to technology: it's like when you used to record a cassette message on your home answering system. You didn't have to erase the other message, you just recorded on top of it. So embracing a new belief is like that: recording on top of the old outdated views or words you used to believe.

A vision board created only of visuals melds together to represent a turning point of international opportunity for Lauren George.

What I Believe About Myself

I believe _____

I deserve _____

I am _____

From this moment on I discover _____

I am grateful I have _____

S = Share

The creation process starts with gratitude and comes full circle with sharing and giving. You connect to the "wisdom-at-large," drawing on what many spiritual leaders call the "universal consciousness" when you share your boards.

If You're Still Having Trouble Pinpointing Goals

If you're having trouble figuring out what you want—what your goals are—look at what you want to do in your life and ask why. Think about the top things you want to experience. For many people, this is a much more effective tactic than pinpointing their goals. Wisdom leader Lee Brower, founder of Quadrant Living LLC and one of the teachers in *The Secret,* agrees that for many people complex goal setting and massive lists of goals may be a waste of time. In fact, goal lists may stop them from living the life they want to live. For many of us, goals imply the *way* to do something and not the *why.*

Focus on the top five experiences you want to create in your life. Phrase them all in the positive versus overcoming something negative. Try to look at several aspects of your life: health, fitness, income streams, relationships, and lifestyle.

As an example, here are my top five experiences:

1) Create and promote this book so it is listed in the top 10 of the *New York Times* best-seller list (notice how specific I am getting here).

2) Increase my fitness level and my endurance strength (notice how this is phrased as a positive versus saying "get back into shape" or "lose 10 pounds").

3) Travel to an exotic place (not just travel or trips, but exotic places, a phrase from my childhood when I used to imagine life beyond the city street we faced, with buses and trucks heading to highways beyond).

4) Enhance my life with faithful and fun new friends.

5) Live surrounded by nature and beauty.

So what if your vision is outlandish, that you dream of living back in ancient Egypt. Maybe you still want to be a princess. Go ahead and create a board or a part of a board that appears to be total fantasy (suspend disbelief). Parée Eagleton had a friend Photoshop her with her red "princess" dress onto an Egyptian scene and added some red hearts for romance. Who knows where it may lead her in life. It's a great vision though; perhaps a reminder that life is not linear. Maybe a trip down the Nile will re-instill passion into your life!

Next Steps: Take a look at the experiences. What aspects do you already manifest or have you created in your life? If I look at my top five list, number five is true already. I look out on boats and a marina and see the sun rise and set from my patio. So of course, what makes the most sense is to acknowledge that experience and be grateful for it. Rather than removing it from my list I keep it there to reinforce my good fortune and to see how I can experience it at a deeper level; for example, by taking morning and evening walks. Even on my busiest days I can do this. Even before I create a new vision board, I start to receive the benefits of being in the flow and recognize that my vision is already in process.

Ways to Create Your Vision Boards

There is no one right or wrong way. The exercises and sequences recommended here have worked successfully for many people, but feel free to be creative as you proceed.

Individual Creations

Individuals can share and give by joining online forums, by attending law of attraction meet-ups, or by showing friends and family how to create vision boards.

Group Creations

Some people like to create their first vision boards or a first vision board for each new year, often called an annual vision board, during a workshop or class. That way they can discuss their ideas and get input and moral support. By having an expert vision board facilitator guide them through the process, they feel more at ease and find the structure enables them to complete their boards by the end of the workshop.

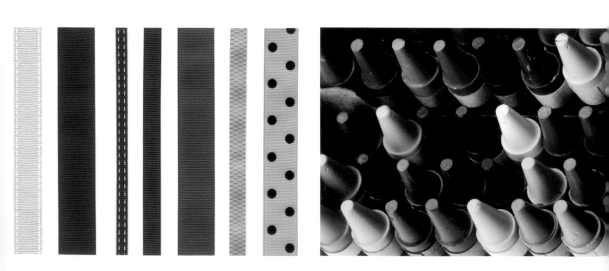

Creating a Vision Board Step by Step

The following list outlines the steps to creating your vision board.

1. Collect your notes from your visioning experience and vision statement and review them.

2. Focus on creating from the inside out, which will help you get into the right mind-set for creating your vision boards.

3. Get into the flow. Eliminate distractions, add some music, if that helps, and carve out some time for your vision board creation so you can enjoy it.

4. Gather together the basics that you'll need to create your board:

- magazines or other images or access to a computer with a printer where you can search for images to download and print out

- scissors and/or a paper cutter

From your children's crayons to ribbons, twine, and snips of fabric, add color and impact so that your inner eye will be attracted to manifest your visions. (iStock)

Advantages of group creation:

✦ it can be empowering;

✦ a trained facilitator can coach you to your best vision;

✦ the set time of the workshop, webinar, or class provides structure to encourage completion in one cycle of a day or a few hours or evenings;

✦ appreciation flows when the class or workshop is led by a supportive coach;

✦ there are more goodies to share—more magazines to choose from, different kinds of glue or paste to try, lots of sparkle and embellishments, like stickers, to add to your board.

- posterboard or other mounting space picked out (some people like to paste directly onto a wall or to the top of a desk or table or even on the front of a dresser)

- glue or glue stick, or other adhesive that is not dried out. Most people ask more about what glue or paste to use than what to put on their boards. I prefer spray adhesive; other artists like a glue stick or rubber cement. It depends on the size and thickness of your images. Just be sure you like the arrangement of elements before you start gluing them to the board.

5. Tap into your own creative style. Here's where some people prefer to be guided, to have me prompt them to sketch out the sections for their boards—which section should be for romance or which for wealth—or help them to figure out what the feng shui of the board is. But if you're using my system, you will probably create more than one board and you will do it your own way.

6. Try starting at the center and working outward, which is one option when creating your board. It is the traditional method used in the art of collage. But I've created boards where I put on four or five major images and then surround those with phrases, power words, or inspirational sayings (or affirmations).

7. Overlap pictures, tear the images out of magazines, zigzag the edges; among the vision boards in this book, you'll see that many of the most interesting ones are those where the images overlap.

8. Embellish with your own touches. Many of the boards in this book combine drawings, magazine pages, photographs, and sketches with accents such as stickers, glitter, beads from an old necklace, bottle caps, or even sections of old paintings or fabric pieces. By incorporating them into a collage, overlapping images, adding another picture or portion of an image on the top of that, you create a design that draws you to look at it again and again. Don't worry: you can always add other embellishments like ticket stubs or sticky notes to vary a more traditional collage with photos or images lined up in rows.

Getting into the Vision Board Flow

Creating vision boards is a process that puts you in the flow; it's natural. Most scientists define "flow" as the mental state in which a person is fully immersed in what he or she is doing and actually feels energized, focused, involved, and successful during the process. Being in the flow is used to explain those times when you lose your own sense of self-consciousness. Mihály Csikszentmihályi, author of *Flow: The Psychology of Optimal Experience,* describes flow as "being completely involved in an activity for its own sake. The ego falls away. Time flies. Every action, movement, and thought follows inevitably from the previous one, like playing jazz. Your whole being is involved, and you're using your skills to the utmost." Athletes call this "being in the zone."

Think back. Did time ever fly for you when you were doing an activity, such as reading, riding your bike, knitting, or backpacking? Chances are you were "in the flow" at that point.

How can you get in the flow for creating your vision board?

+ Understand the goal of your board (to clarify or make "real" your vision).

+ Realize this is your board—there is no right or wrong way to create it.

+ Think about how satisfying it will be to see this visual depiction of your vision. It will indeed be like a dream come true that you can then turn over to the universe and continue to receive benefits from.

If You're Stuck

For some of my clients who just can't get started on their own vision boards, I suggest they begin their journeys by creating a vision board for their favorite charity or nonprofit organization or for a social cause they believe in. Some topics can include "end hunger," "free Tibet," "stop domestic violence," and "peace please." No matter what the cause, make sure your spin on it is positive—your vision board is not meant to be a personal rant or critique of the world around you.

Many people describe the process as soothing. The apparent simplicity of creating a vision board is deceptive because the experience truly empowers inspired action and provides you with a tangible touchstone: it shows you what it will look like to realize your visions.

Vision Board FAQs

(Frequently Asked Questions)

1. What goes on a vision board?

Visuals, affirmations, favorite quotations, power words, and any embellishments you want to add to attract and continue to encourage you to focus your attention on your board. Embellishments include such elements as stickers, postage stamps from other countries, ticket stubs, glitter, beads, bottle caps, ribbon, lapel pins, business cards, flowers (dried and silk), leaves and other natural elements—whatever enables you to envision your best possible future.

2. What size should a vision board be and what materials should it be made from?

Size: Most people choose to make their vision boards by hand on poster or chipboard that is approximately 18 x 22 inches. Many prefer boards that have styrofoam backing because they are sturdier. There are also software vision board kits that produce files that can be adapted into screensavers and even ported to your cell phone for wallpaper. By scanning your handmade board you can add a digital spin to your visions too. Many of my clients choose to downsize their vision boards with a smaller scan that they can either carry with them or post at their desk or even in their car. I've even seen wallet-size versions of boards and of course iPhone- and Blackberry-size replicas.

Materials: Photographs, vintage postcards, architectural drawings, stickers, stamps and foil stars, bugle beads, rhinestone decorations, and even ribbon add a personalized touch. But I've seen such unusual objects as old phonograph records, sea glass, shells, vintage medals, and even labels from brand products and logos from companies that people want to work with.

3. What types of images/visuals should I use and where do I find them?

Bright, simple images seem to work best, and I suggest no more than eight to ten major images per board. You can find images everywhere—in old magazines, in your own photo albums, in your holiday memory box, and at vintage stores, garage sales, and art shows. Don't hesitate to ask an artist to personalize a painting or a sketch for you. Showcase it at the center of your creation or complement your board with a defining image display that's

A Happy Birthday vision board, like this one by Annie Kaycora, brightens anyone's special day, no matter how old the person is. Plus you can have your cake and eat it too if you affix a digital image of your actual cake to the center of the board. Promise—no calories added to your hips.

more appropriate for your cubicle. Vintage images are available copyright-free online and in scrapbook and hobby stores. Searching online for images? Consider going to www.flickr.com and looking for images that are marked "Creative Commons," which means that the photographer or artist agrees that you can use his or her image without permission and without paying a fee.

4. What kind of adhesive should I use?

Some artists swear by glue sticks, while others prefer white paste or even colorful thumbtacks or spray adhesive. Let your fingers do the walking and experiment with the design and format of your board and different kinds of images and methods of displaying them on your board.

5. What's the perfect design for my board?

There is no one perfect design for your board. Overlap images, tear your pictures into strips, copy your favorite poem and add it to the mix. Some feng shui experts like to follow that particular system, while other artists find that just posting a few well-chosen pictures on their boards manifests faster because their focus is concentrated on those few images.

6. How big should my pictures be?

Most people find that images are most effective when they are at least 6 x 9 inches. Other artists like to add mini-size accents of real-life objects, such as dollhouse chairs, swatches of new carpeting, paint samples, and coins and foreign currency.

7. Should I include my photo on the board?

I encourage my clients to immerse themselves into their visions, and many find this much easier when their pictures are on the board. Seeing themselves living their dreams of driving a race car or working in outreach in India adds emotion and strengthens their intention. It's entirely up to you, though.

8. Why share my board?

We live in a time of renewed community both on- and offline. By sharing in a law of attraction forum or on the Web site for this book, www.ihaveavision.org, you'll attract like-minded people who support your vision. Of course, follow your own intuition. Remain positive about your board. Don't compare it to others; remember your board is special. A perfect response to any comment about your board is "thank you for your input."

9. Should I create my board on my own or with my spouse, lover, or partner?

There are no "shoulds." Many of my clients find that they benefit by creating a joint board and vision and also designing their own special-interest boards for hobbies or their own passions, such as vintage car collecting or fitness. Often parents prefer creating a joint family board and then individual boards for mom and for dad. Your own board reminds you of your independence and adds to self-esteem.

Special Event & Life Celebration Vision Boards

There are several ways to add vision board creation experiences to enhance important events in your life.

Plan a vision board creation session as part of your next family get-together: For this perfect birthday and anniversary celebration activity, ask everyone attending to bring extra copies of his or her favorite pictures of the guest(s) of honor and color photocopies of special momentos relating to the person or couple. Family and friends can sign the back of the board or initial the front. Guests of honor can also create their own boards commemorating the event with help from family and

20 Years from Now · *Activity*

You can do this activity at birthday, graduation, or even anniversary celebrations. The fun part of this is that all you have to do to play is to cut out pictures from magazines that show where you'll be in the next two decades and perhaps even along the way. Keep in mind: Use your power words. Live tomorrow today, and today tomorrow. Create the feeling of twenty years from now in the present. Live in as close proximity to the future as you can.

At the back of this book, or on a separate sheet of paper, write the following. Be sure to use the present tense—it makes the experience more powerful.

Twenty years from now I live in _____.

I am surrounded by _____.

My lifestyle includes _____ and _____.

I center and immerse myself in _____.

My world includes _____ and _____.

On my birthday 20 years from now I feel _____

and _____.

I am grateful for _____ and _____.

friends. (For birthday vision boards, don't forget to take a picture of the cake before the candles are blown out; you can add that photo to the vision board later.) Many of my clients create vision boards as a way to celebrate family holidays; for example, on Thanksgiving Day the sharing starts not only with the potluck preparations in advance but at the table where all of the family and friends gather and share why they are grateful to be there. They include pictures taken that day and downloaded and printed out, as well as drawings and doodles by children and teens at the event.

Design a board in advance as you look forward to an important day, such as an engagement party: The special couple can do this the week or even the night before and then share their vision with the crowd at the event.

Create a board in gratitude after a big event as a way to give thanks for the camaraderie, the décor, and the gifts received: The great thing about creating a gratitude board is that it is the perfect antidote to that after-event wind-down many people experience when a big event is over.

Place a vision board center stage at a community celebration: At First Night celebrations held on New Year's Eve, community leaders and residents join together to create vision boards that are featured in town during the first week in January. Other communities choose to create wish boards on which residents are invited to add their own sticky notes to a public bulletin board or cork wall, creating a wall of wishes.

Valentine's Day Boards: Want to add some family fun to Valentine's Day? Gather several generations of parents, grandparents, and even extended family to create a "vision of love" board. Or invite all your single friends over and provide the materials—including posterboard, magazines, scissors, and glue— so each person can create his or her own relationship vision board.

Here are some other perfect occasions for vision boards: wedding showers, baby showers, graduations, Mother's and Father's Day, retirement parties, family reunions, celebrations of a new job, or preparations for a vacation.

(right) *Artist Peggy S. Pirro created a concept vision board for her coffeehouse even before it opened. Note the tones are almost mocha in color as if she subconsciously was reinforcing the theme and her love for coffee and conviviality!*

The Concept Collage: Another Kind of Visual

If you want to create something other than a vision board, the concept collage is another option. Hollywood and Broadway productions frequently depict the future even before a play premieres worldwide or when the film is still in pre-production. A concept collage or advertising promo mash-up of disparate elements is crafted together to create a defining image of the upcoming production. This same technique can be used to create a concept collage for your new business, vacation home, or other goal in life.

Sometimes a combination of artwork, drawings, and photos is best to depict your future. Concentrating on just one project, such as an upcoming special event—a family reunion, a graduation, a retirement party—can be very powerful. This is also a terrific method to depict an invention or intellectual property, such as a book or film you will produce in the future. Visually portraying an "alternate reality"—beyond what appears to be possible in real life—is Hollywood's forte and is often seen in modern video-game fantasy and role-playing RPMG game images. Consider these as inspiration for your own concept board where you begin to live an alternate future that is your best possible life.

ACTIVATING YOUR VISION BOARDS

Now is the time to make your vision board serve you.
Do you have an old vision board that needs a makeover
or is your new vision board a lemon? In this chapter, you'll
discover how to activate your vision and your vision board
throughout the creation process. You'll also discover the
secrets to activating the pictures on your board. In addition,
I'll explain how your vision board ties in with designing
your ideal day, your ideal lifestyle, and your ideal streams
of income—all part of what has long been known by the
catch-all term "ideal scene."

Without the activation processes and exercises
included in this book, and some of the most
powerful ones are explained in this chapter,
you will not experience the full potential of
your vision and your vision board. Remember,
the goal of the board is not to be a magic wand
but to serve you during your personal journey.

*Speaker and TV personality Marsh Engle invites you to step
into your greatest vision and deepen your web of collaborative
relationships at events like her Amazing Woman's Day. Marsh's
own board features some pretty amazing affirmations and
inspiration for men and women of all ages.*

*May your dreams
call you by name
and when you get
that call give your
hearty response.*

—**Mary Manin Morrissey**

Vision Boards: A Practice Not Just an Activity

All too often people create vision boards in a class, during a weekend workshop, or as an assignment for their jobs. They design them as fast as they can, slapping pictures down using a glue stick that is already dried up, and so the images start falling off even before the board is complete. They make vision boards because their "new age" bosses tell them to or when a partner suggests that all will be changed for the better if they create a vision board together. Then they get frustrated when what's pictured on the board does not happen in the first week.

If you are one of those people with a vision board hanging in the bathroom, stop now and go back and glance again at chapters 1 through 3. Ensure that you are following the recommended sequence of a) visioning your direction/core beliefs; b) following your personal vision statement; and c) designing a board that authentically reflects you and your vision! Creating a vision board is a practice, not just a one-time activity.

For inspiration, you can page through the next three chapters: Relationships, Gratitude, and Wealth and Well-Being. You'll discover how creating a vision board for a special project, a life event, and for different core aspects of your life—work, love, relationships, fitness—may be even more powerful than the massive vision boards that many people designed in the past that are really overview, or panorama, vision boards that give glimpses of the desired lifestyle and life dreams, but don't zero in like a laser on focused visions for each of these areas.

Overview Board Versus Project or Topic Boards

An overview board that covers all aspects of your life and dreams and desires can create a great panorama of your goals and dreams, but for many people it's a bit like looking at the ground from sky high in a plane. You see the key landmarks—mountains, lakes, and houses—but the rest is too blurry to even discern. No wonder people ask why their vision boards are not working for them. When they have a board with hundreds of pictures on it, it's hard for the eyes to focus.

God breaks the heart again and again
and again until it stays open.

– Hazrat Inayat Khan quoted in
The Exquisite Risk by Mark Nepo

How do I make a difference?

I dwell
in
possibility

live.   life.   now.

(left) *Why not keep a "possibility" journal? "I dwell in possibility" is a mantra of Katy Taylor, who shares a favorite quote: "Tell me, what is it you plan to do with your one wild and precious life?" by Mary Oliver.*

(below) *This vision board by Kirsten Stokes clearly reveals that the artist is starting to picture her new reality as a professional photographer (her image is reflected).*

MYSTIC

spirit

Fortune

Oak tree it...

Stay close to nature,
it will never fail you.

someone you

LOVE

free your
Spirit

magic

Practice with Pleasure

DEVILISHLY GOOD

How do you make your vision board serve you? No, it doesn't come with an instruction manual nor does it come with a recipe book, but this chapter will provide you with some tools and techniques that I use and recommend to get the fullest value from your vision board now and in the future.

This chapter will cover such vision board activators as:

- **Affirmations:** Discover the power of positive self-affirmations (phrases, statements, words, and quotes said or written in the first person); they encourage you to stay positive and overcome any negativity. This section will feature excerpts from Dilbert creator Scott Adams. He is a big fan of affirmations.

- **Visualization:** Learn how picturing yourself doing something can be a powerful way to realize your dreams and goals.

- **Feng Shui:** Use the tips from Marie Diamond, one of the teachers in *The Secret*, to get the most out of your vision board.

Vision boards come in all shapes and sizes. (above) The round "possibility portrait," by Pamela Moss—a virtual quilt—is a stunning example of how to celebrate yourself and remember who you are.

(left) Aysha Griffin's overview vision board delves into her revitalized career as a writer and also looks at travel, lifestyle, and relationships. She remembers to keep the images bold and beautiful!

Affirmations for the Twenty-First Century

Affirmations are carefully selected words and phrases that continue to gain and maintain your attention and to "tell" your subconscious mind that your visions are your new reality. Using affirmations certainly helps you focus on the individual visions or goals pictured on your vision board. Positive attention fuels and expresses your subconscious intention to realize your new reality of experiencing those goals in your daily life. You move beyond hoping, wishing, daydreaming, and magical thinking and are propelled by optimism and possibility.

How Dilbert Creator Scott Adams Uses Affirmations

On his Web site, Scott Adams, the creator of the comic strip Dilbert, has often written about his positive experiences with writing affirmations. In Adams's view, the practice seems to work much of the time, and presumably this is not because of any magic. Adams points out that one probable explanation for why affirmations work is that focusing on your visions and actually repeating phrases that relate to your goals actually changes your perspective.

Adams says he used affirmations to achieve several of his major life goals, one of which was to become a syndicated cartoonist—not just cartoonist but syndicated, meaning newspapers and other media would send his cartoons around the world for him. Fifteen times a day, every day for six months, he wrote out:

"I, Scott Adams, will become a syndicated cartoonist."

I advise my clients that it's not enough to be in the right time and right place; you have to recognize it when you are. I always say you need your antenna up to receive the right frequency. Says Adams, "I can imagine affirmations tuning a person in the same way, until it seems that extra luck is being provided by the universe, but all that's happening is that it's more easily recognized."

He also notes that each time an affirmation results in a vision, goal, or dream being realized, it increases a person's optimism level. We've all had days or weeks or even years when it seems like everything just goes right, and we feel like we have the "Midas touch" to make anything turn into gold.

For me, it's anytime I go on vacation. I always know there is a guardian angel watching out for me and I seem to handle

Affirmations Aloud

Some people prefer to say their affirmations aloud. Feng shui expert Marie Diamond suggests actually saying your affirmations in front of your vision board and talking to your vision board. It is a technique that reminds me a bit of gardeners who have great luck talking to their plants.

any setback, like a plane delay or ticket change, as another part of the adventure. You might say that it is simply looking at the experience in a more positive way. But I believe that it ties into an ongoing affirmation that I believe "I am my best possible person when I'm on vacation!" My newest affirmation is "Every day is like a vacation for me and I am my best possible person today just as I am when I vacation!"

Why Affirmations Are Important

The best affirmations:

+ are healing, positive scripts you create or adopt to counter negativity;

+ are quotes or statements that you find or create that free you from opinions of the past or counter any opposition you may get from your family/peers as you head toward your visions;

+ aid in visualization of new systems and put order in your life even before you've achieved it physically;

+ are empowering—you create them, you say or write them, and they are highly personalized to your envisioning exercises;

+ are a bit like watering your garden each day; they give you permission to grow and change.

Subliminal and Paraliminal Messages

A **subliminal** is a signal or message embedded in another medium, designed to pass below the normal limits of perception. Experts say that these messages, or in this case affirmations, are unrecognizable by the conscious mind but in many cases can impact the subconscious deeper mind and our own attitudes and actions. There are systems that allow you to combine your affirmations with your favorite song tracks, thus adding a "subliminal" and additional audio track to the music.

A **paraliminal** is a new delivery system for audio and video that supposedly targets both the left and right sides of the brain. A company called Learning Strategies creates audio and video CDs and DVDs that provide different messages to each side or to your headphones. It sounds confusing, but for many people this is an extremely effective method to encourage new thought and action patterns. In a way it sounds to me like it almost "tricks" your mind into grabbing onto the new. It's certainly worth checking out.

What You Can Do with Affirmations

Here are more guidelines about this self-empowering and inspirational technique that changes outdated lifelong practices or life scripts that are not working for you.

✦ Say your affirmations aloud or mouth them silently, depending on where you are.

✦ Write them in a journal—most affirmation practitioners still insist on the power of handwriting versus typing. Maybe it's the mind-body connection, but the combination of pen and paper seems to activate both the right and left sides of the brain and produces more impact in your conscious and subconscious mind.

- Record them and listen to them daily using a video or audio recorder or your computer's microphone input and speaker output.

- Experience next-generation affirmation delivery by doing exercises that focus on subliminal or paraliminal delivery via software screensavers or enhanced musical tracks.

- Employ the age-old Eastern practices of meditation combined with mantras, variations of phrases, or repeated words that relax you and put you into what's called an alpha brain-wave state where you're more in touch with your subconscious and your inner spirit.

- Use self-hypnosis to reinforce affirmation power.

(opposite left) *Who says a vision has to be on a board? Called Delicate Vision of Peace, this board by Joy P. Choquette features a recycled album cover and old sheet music on a round base that can be hung as a reminder that visioning is an ongoing process reinforced by affirmations of peace and goodwill.*

(left) *One of the most famous affirmations in the world, explored by Theda Sandiford in this vision board, is "I am woman."*

Affirmation Formats

Many times my clients want me to be more specific about how to create and use affirmations. The first step is to look at some affirmations and see how they can empower you.

I divide affirmations into three categories—I am, I can, and I will—as do the experts at Coping.org, a Web site that provides information for people who are dealing with stresses in their lives. The following are some examples of affirmations; there are more on the organization's Web site as well. Phrase your affirmations in the present tense to really feel like you are receiving and/or have received the result already rather than the result being some distant goal.

No words are necessary in this vision board that symbolically urges its creator, Theda Sandiford, to acknowledge her winning ways.

"I Am" Statements

Personally, I like to use affirmations even when I cannot suspend my conscious belief that something is happening or will happen to me for some ingrained reason from the past. In that case, I add a gerund, meaning an "ing" ending, to the affirmation: I am losing weight, I am living in Paradise, and so on.

I am energetic.
I am strong.
I am enthusiastic.
I am intelligent.
I am relaxed.
I am beautiful.
I am joyful.
I am a good person.
I am trusting.
I am caring.

I am generous.
I am loving.
I am courageous.
I am smart.
I am forgiving.
I am creative.
I am open.
I am talented.
I am sharing.

"I Can" Statements

Many experts see "I can" as a statement of your potential. For some people, that phrase works well as a jumpstart to begin visualization. The phrase "I can" reinforces your belief that you can change, and it also amplifies the desire to help yourself.

I can lose weight.
I can grow.
I can stop smoking.
I can heal.
I can handle my children.
I can let go of guilt.
I can gain self-confidence.
I can let go of fear.
I can take risks.
I can change.
I can be a winner.

I can be positive.
I can be strong.
I can be a problem solver.
I can pass my test.
I can handle my own problems.
I can laugh and have fun.
I can be honest with my feelings.
I can be assertive.
I can let go of being compulsive.
I can control my temper.
I can succeed.

"I Will" Statements

Many affirmation practitioners promote what's called a "success prophecy"—"I will" statements—with which you predict your own success to encourage your present vision and focus in on your priorities. I see "I will" as a phrase that gets you to "I am," if you absolutely cannot say or write "I am." It's a bit like deciding if you want more pepper or salt with your dinner; it's a personal preference that has to "feel" right to you.

I will like myself better each day.
I will gain emotional strength each day.
I will lose weight each day.
I will smoke less each day.
I will control my temper today.
I will give others responsibility for their lives today.
I will grow emotionally stronger each day.
I will smile more at my customers today.
I will offer my comments in class today.
I will praise my children today.
I will feel good things about myself today.
I will sleep easily tonight.
I will feel less guilt each day.
I will face my fears courageously today.
I will take on only what I can handle today.
I will take care of myself today.
I will challenge myself to change today.
I will manage my time better today.
I will handle my finances wisely today.
I will take a risk to grow today.

Affirmation Mirrors

Throughout this book I reinforce the practice of mirroring your affirmations and your visions in different locations and in different physical manifestations.

Index cards, sticky notes, and mailing labels or file-folder labels can be posted anywhere and are easily added or removed. They can feature words, phrases, or statements to remind you of your positive self-affirmation exercise in progress. For people who are into text messaging, mobile affirmations may be the way to go.

Consider posting your affirmations in unusual places where you will see them throughout your day: mirrors in your house, the dashboard in your car, the refrigerator door, the back of your mobile phone, in your wallet, on the printout of your "to-do" list. Many clients like to include affirmations on their desktops or as part of their laptop screensavers so that a small balloon pops up and opens to their affirmations—finally, a pop-up that you can be happy to see onscreen!

Visualization

This is the practice of "seeing yourself doing something," even when you are not doing it. It is especially helpful when you are trying something new, or want to instill a new positive habit to replace a negative one.

Visualizing with Defining Images

This is where the defining images on your vision boards have the most impact. It may be a picture or an object (a sign, a piece of jewelry, a sculpture, or a painting) that brings the vision to life for you.

To make the most of a defining image, try the following exercise:

✦ Get into a relaxed state. Add a bit of music or go into a room where there are no distractions. Maybe step outside into your garden or backyard, if you have one.

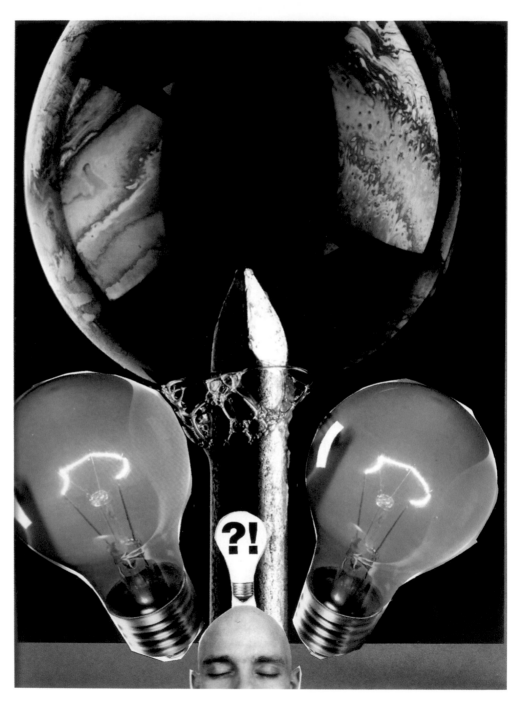

Did you know the human body can power a city for a day? This vision board, called Explain, reminds the artist, Theda Sandiford, of her own personal energy, even when she's fatigued.

- Be prepared to do this for at least twenty minutes each day for one to six months.

- Be sure your defining images are in place on your vision board and then mirrored in other locations—in your home office, in your car, on a keychain you carry with you.

- Start with gratitude for having the time to do this affirmation exercise and actually experiencing the feeling and vibration of having what you are affirming.

Checking Out the Future: Jim Carrey and $10 Million

One of the most famous Hollywood visualization anecdotes is about comedian Jim Carrey and the $10 million check he wrote to himself long ago. It was 1987, and the then twenty-five-year-old Canadian comic was struggling to make his way in show business. One night he drove his old Toyota up to the top of Mulholland Drive in the Hollywood Hills and looked out at the glitter on the Los Angeles lights. Sitting there dreaming about his future wasn't enough; he wanted to really *see* it! So he pulled out his checkbook and wrote himself a check for ten million dollars. He dated the check Thanksgiving 1995 and added the notation "for acting services rendered." Note how specific he was in this visualization: a) he wrote $10 million, not just "tons of money"; b) it was time-sensitive, "Thanksgiving 1995"; c) he spelled out his "what" by adding very clearly in the notation "for acting services rendered"; d) the *how* wasn't his problem.

This story stands out because Jim Carrey's expression of what some would have called "brazen optimism" turned out not only to come true but to be conservative! By 1995, Carrey had already acted in *Ace Ventura: Pet Detective, The Mask,* and *Dumb & Dumber,* which had yielded worldwide grosses of $550 million.

He carried that check around with him for years. On *The Oprah Winfrey Show,* he explained it by saying, "I wrote myself a check for ten million dollars for acting services rendered and dated it Thanksgiving 1995. I put it in my wallet and it deteriorated. And then, just before Thanksgiving 1995, I found out I was going to make ten million dollars for *Dumb & Dumber.* I put that check in the casket with my father because it was our dream together."

(right) *Take a closer look at words like "inspired" on this piece by Katy Taylor. See that they can have a second meaning that will truly awaken your potential.*

Feng Shui and Your Vision Board

Many of my clients want to know where to place their vision boards for maximum effect. So I decided to go to the expert, feng shui guru Marie Diamond, who is also a star of the movie *The Secret*. Diamond reveals her top tips for getting maximum success from your vision board, as well as other exercises connected with the law of attraction.

Vision Board Placement Tips

◆ Always place it somewhere you can see it: in your office, your bedroom, or your living room.

◆ Place it where there is beautiful energy; don't hide it in your bathroom or in your closet.

◆ Be sure to place it where there is action and where there is life.

◆ Be sure to place it at eye level so you can focus on it, for example, above your bed or where you sit when you dine.

Diamond promises that by practicing double happiness—inner happiness within you and outer happiness in your environment—you will improve your destiny and attract your greatest dreams. Improve how you think, feel, and act, and you will improve your destiny. Improve your home, and you will think, feel, and act differently.

(left) *Aras Bauskauskas,* Survivor: Exile Island's *one-million-dollar first-place winner, notes that accepting the abundance of the big check was tougher than winning the TV show challenges. Today he is creating a yoga retreat as a living affirmation.*

Colors and Vision Boards

Diamond believes that using certain colors in different areas of boards that focus on such topics as success, health, relationships, and wisdom can strengthen the manifestation process.

■ Success: royal blue is helpful in manifesting professional success.

■ Health: emerald green helps manifest good health in body, mind, and spirit.

■ Relationships: the color rose is helpful in manifesting great relationships.

Wisdom: yellow is helpful in manifesting wisdom and knowledge.

Diamond's Biggest Secret

———————◆———————

In fact, Diamond says the biggest secret of all personal development is in improving the feng shui and positioning of your vision board within your home. Changing your destiny and changing your thoughts and feelings can take many years of practice. Improving your home is the easiest of all. Changing your bed, changing pictures, changing the flow can be done in a couple of minutes.

More Ways to Activate Your Vision Board

In addition to affirmations, visualization, and feng shui, there are a number of other techniques my clients use to make their vision boards serve them better—from journal writing to sharing their dreams and goals with others as if they have already been realized or are being realized. Here's a quick list of several other methods that I encourage my clients to explore to make their vision boards serve them better:

✦ **Create Vision and Gratitude Journals:** Self-help guru Tony Robbins says a life that is worth living is worth writing about. Even if you don't write in your journal every day, it's still a great resource when the going gets tough and gives you a chance to counter the mind-cluttering thoughts that may be holding you back. Note that a journal is not a diary—you should not use it just to record activities, it should be a self-exploration exercise.

✦ **Keep a Journal of the Future:** One of my clients keeps a journal of her future, already living her visions virtually. Or create one of our most popular types of vision boards, called "20 Years from Now." You can vary it to be six months or one year, or put a specific date on your board.

✦ **Live Your Vision Virtually:** A fun way to experience this in the online world is to create a room, house, or life experience you are yearning for in a virtual world, like www.secondlife.com.

✦ **Express Your Positive Thoughts Publicly:** Seek support in an online forum or community bulletin board and share your positive outlook and feelings. Don't use these online resources just to complain. If you do

What will the next twenty years hold for you? This father's "Vision of the Future" is filled with family, prosperity, a trip to Spain, and other travel plans. You are the co-creator of your own life!

you'll regret it because your negative thoughts are then captured for posterity. No one wants to read about what a lousy day it was yesterday five years from now. There's real value in expressing positive affirmations!

✦ **Surf for Your Vision:** Cap off your affirmation exercise each day with a period of ten minutes of Web surfing into your vision. Visualizing about living in a summerhouse in Cape Cod this July? Research places to rent online; you'll be one step closer to realizing your vision. Post your plans on your Facebook profile. Go ahead and be brave; just write that you are living in Cape Cod this summer in the little window on the site that asks what you are doing now. Maybe July is a long way off, but by posting that positive statement, you may get a brief email or text from a long-lost friend, or the sister of a friend might write that she has another share in her summerhouse available and ask if you want it.

✦ **Practice Your Affirmations in Real Life:** I often encourage my clients to try out their new life in advance by talking with random people they meet during the day. When you stop by the dry cleaner and he asks you what's new, go ahead and say, "I am getting thinner every day." See how it feels. No doubt he'll give you a compliment that encourages you. If you're sitting next to someone on a train or a plane, talk about your planned vacation as if it were happening tomorrow not months from now and see how excited you get about it. Who knows, you could end up with a referral for a place to stay, which will get you there faster than saving for hotel expenses.

RELATIONSHIPS

This chapter focuses on relationships of all kinds—
from the one you have with yourself to those with a
partner, family, and friends. The good news is that a
vision board can serve you in every aspect of your
relationships: from helping you to visually picture
your own quest to love yourself to enabling you to
design visions of romance or partnership.

The law of attraction assures us that we have the power to
create our own successful relationships, despite our past
history, our physical appearance, or our family patterns
and conditioning. We can love and be loved now and
forever! A vision board that focuses on love allows you
to tap into your ongoing self-discovery, or what is called
"heartwork," rekindling your relationship with your own
soul and heart's desires.

Art by Pamela Moss

*The best kind of
love is the kind that
awakens the soul,
makes us reach for
more, plants a fire in
our hearts, and brings
peace to our minds.*

**—from the film
The Notebook**

Breaking Outdated Relationship Cycles: Naava Piatka's Story

The opportunity to create a new reality is one we all experience every morning. Yet, all too often, my clients cling to relationship patterns that aren't working anymore. Naava Piatka was one of those people; today, she embraces a renewed relationship with herself and lives her future today.

For twenty-two years, Naava had been a stay-at-home mother of three in suburban Boston, juggling roles as a part-time artist/actress/writer. It is no wonder that after enduring a lengthy, conflict-ridden divorce fraught with constant court battles over money, Naava desperately wanted to break free from her past and create a new reality for herself. "I had spent most of my life as a caretaker and dependent, and worrying over finances." Now it was time to focus on personal dreams of creative success, accomplishment, and personal fulfillment. One step in the process was moving to New York City.

Going from living a family-oriented life to being single was no easy feat. "I took a leap of faith, downsized my possessions, and upscaled my ambition." More than a physical move, it was a spiritual, transformative journey to reinvent herself.

The value of the "new reality" vision board: Naava created a collage to provide inspiration during the transition time. She chose images representing her desire for financial independence, a loving relationship with a man, a meaningful career and, most importantly, peace and harmony. She shares the affirmations that are tacked to the back of her board:

> *I am calm and composed, trusting in the right timing.*
> *Money is secure and keeps flowing to me.*
> *I am free from money worries and concerns.*
> *I am satisfied, prosperous, and at peace.*
> *I am fully self-expressed.*
> *I am relaxed and surrounded by beauty.*
> *I enjoy exotic vacations with my true love.*

Designing a new reality with pastel blues and bold shades of yellow and gold provides visual symmetry and inspiration for Naava. Her collage depicts her new reality as a Broadway performer and author after twenty-two years of being a stay-at-home mother of three. Today, she lives her vision and offers an inspiring tale through her journey to a renewed sense of self and family.

How Naava pictured and realized her new reality in advance

Many of her visions have already manifested. Her goal is to have a long run of her internationally acclaimed one-woman show *Better Don't Talk!* in New York City. It is about the life of her mother, a Holocaust survivor and the star of the Vilna Ghetto Theatre in Lithuania.

Take a closer look at her board and you can see the emotionally charged images. "A glamour photo of my mom, Chayela Rosenthal, in an evening gown and long black gloves is placed in the center right next to a gold statuette, symbolizing my desired Tony Award. The confident and serene image of actress Julianne Moore holding the watch (she's got the same red hair and freckles as me), keeps reminding me to let go of my impatience."

After creating the board, Naava performed as a guest artist at major cabaret conferences, bought her dream home in New Jersey on a cliff with a beautiful view, found romance on vacation, and completed her father-daughter memoir, *No Goodbyes*, about her charismatic father's dramatic past—he was also a Holocaust survivor—and their relationship.

Her true joy and harmony comes from her newfound spiritual relationship with herself. "I took the time to explore my life anew, alone, releasing past anger, regret, and disappointment. I had to learn to love, honor, and treasure myself first. Now, instead of finding fault, I find grace and gratitude in everything that comes my way. Even my nasty divorce I view as a divine gift. It taught me the art of forgiveness and letting go. The peace and freedom I experience deep within me, well now, that's my true wealth."

Naava's Vision Board

It was designed to serve her during a transition period from divorce to her new reality as a prosperous self-supporting woman actively involved in acting, writing, and pursuing her dreams. She is living out the images of peace and balance in her new life in a townhouse high upon a cliff overlooking the Hudson River and the Manhattan skyline and exploring her newfound relationship with herself, with time for romance along the way. An overview transition board is a great way to create a landscape view of the path ahead.

✦ **Naava's Defining Images:** She incorporates images that are meaningful to her, such as pictures of successful women who serve as role models and a gold statuette that symbolizes the Tony Award in her future, along with an inspirational view of a woman in a chair gazing up at blue skies. Select defining images that are as specific and colorful as the ones that Naava chose.

✦ **Naava's Power Words:** "Peace," "harmony," and "prosperity" are her power words (which she chose not to put on her board). The triad she uses seems to fit all aspects of her new life. Be sure that your power words can fuel you toward your own new reality.

✦ **Naava's Affirmations:** On the back of her board, she combines a series of positive phrases into one meaningful affirmation that focuses her on being calm and trusting that her finances are secure and money is flowing to her. While saying her affirmation she sees herself as prosperous and self-expressed, and she reinforces her role as a star in the theatre world by adding her first and last name when reciting her personalized mantra. This is a great tip for many of my clients who think and hear themselves described as mommy, daddy, grandpa, teacher, or even reverend. It instills a renewed sense of self and vibrates emotionally.

How Naava Uses the GRABS Formula:

Gratitude: She is grateful for her new home, which she calls a sacred space filled with serenity. She is prospering. She daily expresses gratitude for everything in her new life, even the problems and obstacles she views as welcome lessons for self-improvement.

Release and Receive: She discovered that to create her new reality she had to release her past in Boston and receive new opportunities in New York. She let go of her dependency and revels in her newfound independence. She created a more empowered relationship to finances by releasing old resentments, fears, and concerns. She now expects and receives abundance.

Acknowledge and Ask: She takes time to acknowledge her personal and professional accomplishments, and she is discovering answers to what's next in her life by focusing on her family's inspirational heritage. She knows how to ask for what she wants as specifically as possible and accepts guidance.

Be and Believe: She is true to herself and embraces her enriched sense of self-worth. She truly believes that her dreams will come true.

Share: She shares the bounty of her writing, acting, and singing as an "enlightened entertainer," a term she coined to convey the enhanced spiritual element of her various artistic presentations.

Naava's advice: "I hope my vision board inspires others starting a new phase in their lives. First, picture it. Then paste it on a vision board. Then go and passionately and patiently pursue it!"

The Secret to Love

In this chapter you'll see how I encourage people to savor the experience of creating their boards—it is a time for relationship renewal with yourself and others in your life, now and in the future. Inspirational leader Mary Manin Morrissey agrees that there is one core principle for successful relationships of all kinds in our lives—friendship. Morrissey says, "Nurture this single element, and your partnerships, dating, romance, and marriage experiences will blossom the way they are supposed to."

As someone who has relocated at least a half dozen times in my career, from Ohio to New York, San Francisco, Honolulu, the Hollywood Hills, and now to gorgeous Marina Del Rey, California, I know the value of making new friends while keeping the old. A great friendship is priceless.

Enhancing Your Self-Belief and Self-Love

+ **Be sure to include a picture of yourself prominently on your vision board:** Remind yourself that you are the co-creator of your life in addition to any higher power, whether you call him or her God, Allah, or Buddha.

+ **Release the past and false data that you are not worthy of abundance.** Try repeating the favorite mantra of *Survivor* winner Aras Bauskaukas, "I Love Myself, I Love Myself, I Love Myself." Say it a dozen times a day on the hour, and your self-love will get a needed refill.

Being Your Own Best Friend

You may have heard the old adage that it's vital to be your own best friend, but why is it so common that many of us are willing to give up this essential relationship with ourselves in the quest to find that special someone, that promised soul mate, that we lose our very essence of self. The cornerstone of any romantic relationship is having a great relationship with yourself.

Amor est Vitae Essentia,
"Love is the Essence of Life"

How do you know if you're on the right path to a love relationship? To check if you're making the right choices, ask yourself if they are leading you to love. I like the distinction that Mary Manin Morrissey uses: the question to ask is not does this lead to you getting more love but does this path lead to greater loving.

Here's a quick path-to-relationship checkup quiz:

1. Do you have a morning love picker-upper practice? Is there a mantra you say each morning to express your love and gratitude for living?

2. Are you grateful for the good friends you've had in the past? Are you eager to create new relationships today and not wait until tomorrow?

3. Are you ready to release your last ties to your bad relationships and stop complaining this instant?

4. Do you smile when you look at yourself in the mirror?

The more "yes" answers you give, the closer you are to being on the right path.

"To Be" is the title of this handmade doll pin that serves as a portable vision board created by the artist zJayne of Cleveland, Ohio. Art, just like your inner self, sometimes takes its time finding the right audience—you. Affirmation from those around us is only frosting on the cake to those of us who truly appreciate our own talents.

Using Your Vision Board to Meet the Love of Your Life

Diane MacDowall, from the Highlands of Scotland, provides some insight into how she designed a vision board to meet her soul mate, Andy Nicholson, who lived in Austria. MacDowall's board featured images of love, connection, and teaching to create a visual statement. Here are some of her methods for using a vision board.

+ **Picture the two of you together already:** She explains, "When I visualized my perfect soul mate as I made my wish, all I saw in my mind was the two of us lying on a bed together—he was just holding me in his arms, and I felt completely connected."

+ **Create a vision statement for a happy couple:** You are already a happy couple even before you meet that special someone. MacDowall saw and felt herself with Andy Nicholson (whose name she did not know at the time, of course); her vision statement was Happiness . . . Love, Joy, Abundance, Success.

+ **Include pictures of what you want in a mate:** You can be as specific as you want. You might be surprised about who you end up with—perhaps the person you picture on your board.

+ **Step into those images every time you look at the vision:** Immersing yourself in the images virtually is a powerful experience. Remember how Keith Shroyer (chapter 2) began to actually "feel" like he was sailing when he stared at the image of a forty-foot sailboat? You can trust the old "mind over matter" concept to work when you preview your love as if watching a trailer of the film of your life that is about to be created once you are united by the universe.

You may want to consider using some similar guidelines in creating your own vision board to find a relationship.

Meanwhile in Austria...

MacDowall's soul mate Andy Nicholson was preparing to receive and return her visions of love and joy even before they met each other. Two years earlier, at the age of thirty-nine he was in a job rut and holding on to his anger from a failed marriage. This was stopping him from looking at the positive side of

Andy Nicholson created his own mantra that he recites while looking at his vision board several times a day. Each partner can create and design his or her own affirmations that can be recited throughout the day; then in the evening your gratitudes for the day can be said together as a couple.

love and accepting the creation of a new relationship. But then he was inspired to take action and go on a relationship retreat, where he discovered how to design his own personal mantra and power affirmation that allowed him to release his negativity and readied him to receive all the love and joy that MacDowall was visualizing in Scotland.

Andy calls his mantra an incantation.

> *I am Awesome Andy*
>
> *I am Joyous, Healthy, Optimistic, and Passionate*
>
> *I follow my Purposeful and Congruent path, attracting Love, Wisdom, and the comradeship of Kindred Spirits*
>
> *I turn Dreams into Reality, Helping and Inspiring others to do the Same*
>
> *This I do with Gratitude and Appreciation*

It may inspire you to draft a few phrases that you can recite throughout the day while looking at the digital vision board on your computer or when you pass by your relationship board posted on the wall. Nicholson says that the intention for his life is "to be the best I can be, to stop playing small."

Three months after they both set their intention to find a soul mate, they met online. MacDowall had literally just completed her online profile; Nicholson had not been on the "spiritual singles" dating site for several months. While they were both online, Nicholson was drawn to MacDowall's profile. They connected and two days later arranged to meet in London. The rest, as they say, is history.

Marie Diamond's Tips On How to Feng Shui Your Vision for Romance and Relationships

Feng shui master Marie Diamond, featured in *The Secret*, shares eleven tips for making your vision board spark up your romance and relationships.

1. **Picture Yourself Near Your Future Love:** Even on your vision board, you should make sure that you are pictured next to the image of your ideal man or woman. Diamond even suggests that you put a heart around both of you; after all, if you're separate in your vision you may never get together.

2. **Tie In Your Love Affirmations with Romantic Images:** A sample affirmation Diamond shares in her own blog is, "I am grateful that I am in a romantic relationship with a man [or woman] with these qualities" and then name the specifics, such as tall, handsome, blond, athletic, funny, smart, kind, successful, etc. Make sure that you complement the affirmation with images that represent these traits.

3. **Select Images that "Show Emotion":** In addition, create those vibes within you. Be careful when choosing your images of couples. If you want a man or woman who is tender and loving, make sure you find pictures that show a man or woman hugging or with his or her arm around another person (you). Don't select an image of a woman running across the field to the man on the mountain. You may never find your love that way!

(top left) *By creating a love and relationship vision board you can take the mystery out of your future. A Vision Board will help you put the pieces together and take the time to stop and smell the roses and really appreciate the relationships you have and the new ones you are forming. Art by Max Gold.*

(bottom left) *Diane MacDowall and Andy Nicholson both used vision boards to attract their ideal mates, each other, and today they keep their relationship flourishing with their own images of happiness, love, joy, abundance, and success as they live and work together. You can catch a glimpse of the happy couple in the center top row of MacDowall's board.*

4. **Spark Up Your Romance:** Eliminate all water images on your board. Diamond explains that a picture of a couple walking on the beach will not make your relationship hotter. Instead, add an image of a couple by a fireplace or with fireworks in the sky!

5. **Create a Romance-Centered Vision Board:** Add more images with the colors red and shades of pink, and even add a border or frame that is red. If you can't find a frame that shade, you and your lover can paint it together as you design what's next in your relationship.

6. **If You Want to Get Married:** Then make sure the images feature roses; for hot romance, pictures of red flowers will spark up your love life.

7. **Complement Your Romantic Vision Board with Duo-Defining Images:** Every image of people should feature a couple. Also, place two candles together, not three. Pairs of almost any home accessories will underscore your "coupleness."

8. **Add a Couple of Stuffed Animals:** When paired together and placed in your relationship corner, these can symbolize more romance. Add a decorative heart made of rose quartz and entwine it with the legs of the animals.

9. **Frame the Chinese "Double Happiness" Symbol in Red:** Post this symbol in your relationship corner.

10. **Be Sure the Image You Hang Above Your Headboard Is Romantic:** If you're part of a couple already, frame an image of you close together. If you have nothing above your bed, nothing will happen for you romantically.

11. **If You Want More Intimacy or More Sexuality:** Picture that in the photos, paintings, and sculptures that decorate your home.

Why 11 tips? 1 plus 1 equals 2, and two is the number that represents the feng shui of marriage/partnerships, relationships, and giving to each other.

Love makes the world go around, so share your vision of affection with images from hearts to hearth like Lynda Naranjo did in tones of pink, peach, rose, and red. Feng shui expert Marie Diamond says these colors will enhance romance.

LAUNDRY

LOVE

Using Your Vision Board to Celebrate the Love of Your Life

Some couples enjoy creating a vision for their relationship together and others, like Diane MacDowall and Andy Nicholson, simply update the boards they had when they were single and add other practices and rituals to complement those visions still being realized.

Frank Wiegers and Judith Claire, from Santa Monica, California, created a vision board together. Wiegers is an ex-fighter pilot, writer, Science of Mind practitioner, and licensed relationship coach; Claire is an artist, writer, counselor, and coach. They share their insight about relationships in their upcoming book and a seminar series that they have depicted on their vision board. The couple is envisioning a coaching business and their own TV show.

Claire explains the use of vivid colors, "I used red, the color of passion, because it represents the energy center that grounds us on Earth and gives us the foundation for what we're going to do here. Orange, the color of joy, stands for the energy center connected with sex and creativity." Check out the symbols of fire and hearts. Even the power words add a sense of vibrancy and energy that radiate from the vision—"Sacred," "Divine Sex," "True Love"—and complement their vision statement, "Our relationship is a spiritual practice."

Take a closer look at the vision board, and you'll see that they've been careful to add a balance of personal and business images. Their own relationship is fantastic and loving. What an inspiration to find out that he is seventy-three and she is sixty-four.

Together, Wiegers and Claire share some of the personal-relationship preparation work they did before they became a couple. Wiegers, who hadn't dated in two years after the sudden death of his previous partner, had been playing a musical meditation tape by his friend Robert Frey that featured the phrase "I am opening to love" set to music.

Claire had recently told the universe to "just send me the right man, I don't care how old he is," because she felt most of the men who had been approaching her were too young (she was sixty at the time). "Never in a million years did I expect my soul mate to be sixty-nine—nine years older than me," says Claire. She had also made a "firm decision" that her next man would be a relationship genius. "And I got him," she says. They met at the

Frank Wiegers and Judith Claire created a vision board that reflects their relationship—both personal and business.

memorial ceremony for Frey, who was a mutual friend. They kept a positive outlook, and their relationship only got deeper when, after dating for just a bit longer than a year, Claire found out she had cancer. Wiegers stayed by her side through the chemotherapy, and they exchanged vows in February 2008.

What can you learn from their experiences prior to meeting?

✦ Begin your love affirmation in advance of dating.

✦ Be flexible about age, but know what you want.

✦ View your relationship as a spiritual practice with the emphasis on both "spiritual" and "practice."

✦ Once you and your soul mate are together, create your own "couple vision" of what comes next.

Visions of Love and Sex:
5 Tips to Help Spice Up Your Visioning

To find out how a man or woman can be both spiritual and sexy and use his or her vision board to inspire more romance, I turned to my longtime client and colleague Jina Bacarr, a nationally acclaimed romance novelist for Harlequin Enterprises and author of the Reviewers International Organization (RIO) Award-winning erotic novel, *The Blonde Geisha*, for some tips to help readers spice up their vision boards. Bacarr explained that the answer is what she calls erotic meditation, which allows us to explore primal needs to connect on a spiritual and emotional level with body and mind.

In her earlier nonfiction book, *The Japanese Art of Sex*, Bacarr explains that as with the basic law of attraction "you aim to elevate your mood to a heightened sexual awareness, making the practice a perfect prelude to that special encounter with your mate." She advises us that the goal is not to lull ourselves into blissful semiconsciousness but a higher level of involvement.

Bacarr and I created the following five tips to help you use your vision board to put you in the mood.

1. **The scent of a woman is a kiss promised.** Just as the geisha uses aromatherapy to capture the mood of the moment, complement the love power of your vision board by adding scented candles or aromatic oil pots nearby. Your fragrance can transform your mood as well as his. One fascinating female client of mine even glues sample perfume strips with her husband's favorite scent to her romance vision board. Another client applies extra lipstick at the end of the romance vision board creation process and kisses her lover and her board with a big wet smack that seals the experience with an impression that lasts as long as the board does.

2. **Bathing renews the body and the soul.** A bath is your special time to relax and think pleasant, sexy thoughts. Turn your bathroom into a spalike sanctuary by adding Asian accents to your bathing area, such as yellow citron and green moss. Consider creating an additional, slightly spicier relationship vision board that features you and your partner in swimsuits or even nude and post it on the inside of your bathroom door.

3. The art of the tea ceremony creates harmony and balance. During the performance of the tea ceremony, a geisha accepts a sweet cookie before drinking the bitter tea. To aid in visualizing your romantic goals together as a couple, consider beginning a ritual of a late-night teatime every evening. Be sure to have an exotic tea to try along with a favorite sweet cookie—you, of course! Or encourage more balance in your relationship by adding a love visioning session where you whet the appetite for each other by focusing on your vision board and saying sweet nothings. Some couples make it a habit to kiss every time they both pass by their vision board and even add a touch of mistletoe or a kissing (pomander) ball to accent their visions of love.

4. Beauty is all around you if you close your eyes and open your mind. Go on a date and bring home a flower or souvenir, such as a ticket from the opening night of that wonderful play you just saw or a coin from your trip to Mexico, to add to or accent your relationship vision board. Drape a silk scarf artfully around your board as a tip that you're in the mood. Or encourage your man to hang his favorite tie on the corner of the board as a not-so-subtle hint. Add bits of favorite poems to your board and then take turns reading them to each other while the other person closes his or her eyes and really savors the peace, harmony, beauty, and calmness of your relationship.

5. Every breath you take can help you achieve erotic meditation. Just by breathing deeply and taking time to focus on your vision board, you're following the way of the geisha, who is known for her ability to create serenity in everyone she meets. Deep breathing helps reduce tension in your body and delivers more oxygen to your lungs, bloodstream, and muscles. Practice mindful erotic breathing together with your lover while looking at your visions together. It takes some practice but as soon as you inhale, you'll feel your own chest and stomach expand; as you exhale your stomach will shrink. When you take time to breathe properly together, your bodies will be more in sync for other favorite activities.

Magic Moments and Other Love-Enhancing Ideas

One of the most unique relationship practices that Diane MacDowall and Andy Nicholson have created together is a nightly ritual before they go to bed. They ask each other about their magic moments for that day.

What an inspiration to start your own relationship ritual! Call them magic moments or visions of love, and if you are in a relationship be sure to honor these special experiences every night by saying them aloud to your partner or sharing them in your own vision journal or love diary.

The value of a vision journal and also a vision board is underscored by love coach Renee Piane, who says that she visioned the relationship with her husband in her own personal love journal. Later, she used a savvy method of a renewable love contract to carry them through the dating and courtship period to the union of marriage. Today, her own vision board shows how she is moving from being the expert on Rapid Dating workshops to a Real Love counselor with her own television and radio talk shows, and book projects.

- ✦ **Make a Fun Drawing:** Draw a doodle that reminds you of your lover and add it to your vision board with a thumbtack or glue.

- ✦ **Think about What Makes You Happy:** When you think about your lover, what makes you smile? Write it on a sticky note and post it to your board. Share it with him or her tonight.

- ✦ **Look to Nature:** Find an object in nature that you can share with your partner (it might be an acorn, a rock, or a pretty shell) and place it near your vision board to share as a love offering. Think about what you can share tonight.

- ✦ **Keep a Love and Relationship Journal:** Create your own love and relationship journal and place it near your vision board as a reminder to write in it each night. Start now and take a moment to jot down the visions of love that you discovered today.

- ✦ **Refresh Your Vision Boards Daily or Weekly:** Consider taking new photographs—a flock of birds flying in the sky, or a picture of you and your husband out on "date" night—that represent the wonder of relationships. The new images not only update your boards but keep refreshing your relationship too.

- ✦ **Write Love Poems:** Compose fun love poems or love notes for each other and clip them to your vision board with a fun-shaped paper clip—maybe one in the shape of a flower. One of my clients even puts these notes into perfumed envelopes and then seals them with a kiss of her husband's favorite lipstick.

- ✦ **Clip Love Comics:** One client of mine loves to clip out scenes from his favorite daily comics and post them on the board to show his affection for his partner.

Love makes the world go around and a fresh view is always a delightful addition to the board you created together months ago!

Family: One of the Ultimate Gifts

Author Jim Stovall writes in his classic book, *The Ultimate Gift*, that "families give us our roots, our heritage, and our past. They also give us the springboard to our future." It's inspiring to see his main character realize that "family is not as much about being related by blood as it is about relating through love."

As Stovall and I talked via phone, he noted that, "Family is one of life's ultimate gifts. Some people are born into wonderful families. Others have to find or create them. Being a member of a family is a priceless privilege that costs nothing but love."

For many of us, family includes teachers and students, work colleagues, business partners, church or synagogue friends, neighbors, and online pals.

Creating a Family Vision Board

This is a fun activity for the whole family to do together. It is a way to focus on the uniqueness of your family, your goals together, and everything for which you are thankful. Gather your family members, your housemates, your friends—whoever you consider family—and assure them the experience will be fulfilling.

- ✦ Put on some favorite music and have someone sing along or mouth the words. Be outrageous, leave your egos behind, and just have fun. Sure the teens or 'tweens in the crowd may think you are nuts, but then switch roles and have them practice their favorite songs.

- ✦ Pop in an audio recording that will guide you through the process so that you can act and not think while you create.

- ✦ Once the mood is right, ask a fun question such as, "If you had to describe the best thing about our family, what would you say in two or three words?" Note these on a sheet of paper. Those are the beginnings of your family's power words.

- ✦ Next, encourage everyone to buddy up to find great images that reflect these power words. You can use online search engines or glance at the Creative Commons photos that are copyright-free on Flickr or another online photo site. Or you can just bring out the family photo albums and all those images stored in shoeboxes on the shelves and encourage each person to choose two or three favorites.

One of the options for creating family vision boards is to have the artist in your house draw or paint your family. Pamela Moss, who painted this "family possibility portrait," is an artist who creates these types of portraits professionally.

"'Ohana," Hawaiian for Family

'Ohana, the Hawaiian word for family, can be used to mean two kinds of families: one that consists of a mother, father, and their children; another that refers to friends, coworkers, neighbors, pets, or anyone who has meaning in your life. Maybe you've seen the Academy Award–nominated animated movie *Lilo & Stitch*, in which 'ohana is one of the main themes of the film and "family means nobody gets left behind or forgotten." It's delightful to think, as an author, you readers are part of my 'ohana!

Things happen when I walk through doorways.

Katy Taylor's vision collage reminds us that there is always another doorway through which to find love and, bidden or not bidden, love opens paths that you once thought only money or good fortune would make possible.

✦ Now begin to reinforce the GRABS formula by creating a family gratitude or group "Thanksgiving" vision board. No need to wait until November—you can do it in October or in February, too. Most of my clients find that by making their first family vision board experience one that focuses on all that they are thankful for, they are spurred on to create their better tomorrow today.

Visions of a Family

A transplanted Dutch person now living in New Zealand and one of my colleagues, Linda Boertjens has already done some visioning and exploration about how to create her best possible life and love. Step by step, I'll walk you through the images, power words, and affirmations that she chose for her digital vision board, which she uses as a screensaver and wallpaper on her computer. Scan your handmade board or take it to a copy shop or create your own digital version so that you can do the same.

Linda Boertjens' Vision Board

No matter what your relationships are, you can have multiple vision boards in addition to a couples and family vision board. Linda Boertjens' vision board enables her to live a balanced life as mother, wife, and successful entrepreneur. The board reveals the following:

+ **Her Dream Lifestyle:** Linda explains that the focus of her board is on creating a dream lifestyle, which means freedom, balance, family time, and relaxation. Her vision board shows all of those elements and encourages her to be an example for her children by eating healthy foods. Her visions emphasize quality time with her husband Cornelis and her son Oliver and include pictures showing them all happy together. She believes that doing things as a family will help her son grow into a happy, confident person.

+ **Her Need to Find Time to Relax:** As a busy mom and partner in a thriving home business, Linda knows the value of creating time in her own life to relax, get pampered, and replenish. Her affirmation "I am in balance" really feels good to her. She explains that to be an all-around happy person—as well as mom, wife, and business partner—she realizes it is important to be a happy you. Have a photo taken on a day when you are peaceful and grateful. You'll find that including that photo on your board will generate those same emotions every time you see it.

+ **The Importance of Her RV:** Owning an RV that will allow them to spend time away from the city together and explore nature is an important goal, so she includes that image. Since she's pregnant with

Getting your vision board to serve you and your family:

✦ Create a digital vision board and set it up as your family's computer screensaver so that the vision wallpaper pops up periodically during the day to remind everyone that life is not all work.

✦ Print out a version of your digital vision board and post it somewhere central in your home so that you and your family members can focus on it in the morning and evening.

✦ Really get into your board when you look at it, so that internally you generate the feelings that you will have when these goals become a reality. See yourself living your dream lifestyle now.

✦ Practice being grateful on a daily basis. Turn gratitude into a game by looking for opportunities to help your family members and others. By giving you gain a sense of abundance and peace and empower the law of attraction in return.

her second child, she's been visualizing a pampering couples' tropical holiday for her and her husband, so that image was a must on the newest vision board. Linda explains that she deliberately chose the words "I deserve to" because she continues to work on the belief that she does deserve holidays and pampering.

✦ **Her Desire to Live in Two Places:** Since the Boertjenses emigrated from The Netherlands to New Zealand, one of Linda's biggest goals is for the family to live in Holland three months of the year and skip winter in New Zealand. So images of family in Holland went onto her board along with a special picture of her dad walking with her son, which she says creates a feeling of love and an even stronger desire to make this goal a reality.

✦ **Her Life and Business Partnership:** More couples are starting their own businesses together, sharing work and life. To aid in focusing on the family's business success so that it is also personally rewarding, Linda places three images together on the vision board: an image of a champagne bottle popping alongside a man with his arms raised in excitement; next to this is a vision of the fantastic home she yearns to see her family live in.

Linda Boertjens' vision board helps her create balance in her busy life.

From Vision to Reality: Boertjens' Second Child and Much More

One of the images formerly on Linda Boertjens' personal vision board is no longer there because it became a reality less than three months after it was added to the board: Linda pregnant with her first baby, their toddler Oliver. She updated that by including an accompanying affirmation, "I am now pregnant with a healthy little girl." She visualized herself with a baby and Oliver with a healthy sibling. The fact that they are actually having a girl is a bonus.

What Else Has Manifested for the Boertjenses

Linda Boertjens and her husband Cornelis set up their own business two years ago, and it is growing and allows them both to work from home and choose their own hours. She's even worked it out with Cornelis so both of them look after their son for two days each week, giving them quality time with their son and also continuing their own personal growth.

The family is already experiencing the ability to live in two different places during the year. Because their business is operated on the Internet, they were able to go to their homeland, The Netherlands, for ten weeks last year and work from Holland. And the couple's holiday vision came true with a fantastic Fiji excursion for twelve days.

Creating a Parent and Child Board Together

Divorced or separated parents can keep "mommy and me" or "daddy and me" vision boards in their homes for when their children come to visit. Children will look forward to seeing the shared visions and activities represented on the boards.

Some of my clients who are single parents believe that joint vision boards created with their child or children can have special benefits that no other exercise can instill. It's also perfect while waiting for the birth of a second or third child as a way to make the older children feel special before and after the birth of the new family member.

Update your board weekly with stickers and crayon drawings or stamps. Be sure to include smiley faces so that you can feel the love vibes zapping out from those visuals to you and your child. Styles can vary—they might be fun, easygoing crayon and magazine creations or more formal vision collages that start with cut-out images and then are enhanced with acrylics or pastels.

When children and parents create joint vision boards together it:

✦ provides a stronger bond of love and a joint vision for their future;

✦ helps the child believe that the parent will be there for him or her in the future even if the mom and dad are divorced;

✦ is a low- or no-cost experience that can be relived each day.

These mother-daughter boards were created by Beth Greer and her ten-year-old daughter. Greer, former Learning Annex president and author of Super Natural Home *(Rodale, 2009), made her first vision board at a women's weekend retreat. Her daughter was immediately intrigued when she saw it and said she wanted to make one. They look at their boards daily and are inspired by the imagery and the message to stay positive.*

share the belief

A

It's a wonderful life!

r

t

such a loving place

I

Gift from the Heart

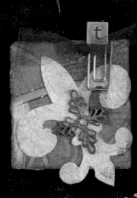

t

u

U

grat·i·tude \'grat-ə-,t(y)üd\ n [ME, fr. M gratitude, fr. L gratus grateful] : the : THANKFULNESS

d

E,

Gratitude
by Renée Tray

GRATITUDE

Develop an attitude of gratitude starting with you—you are worth it! Take a moment right now and look at yourself—your hands, your feet, and your face—with the same kind of admiration you might bestow on one of the most precious sculptures in the Louvre Museum in Paris. Think about this: you are irreplaceable, which makes you priceless!

Far too many people view gratitude as something given to others, and all too often in our society, self-admiration and self-appreciation are viewed as being, well, selfish. Yet it is an unabiding sense of wonder and awe for life that fills us with positive energy so that we can keep in tune with an attitude of gratitude, no matter what happens or what anyone says to us. It's our own self-respect that enables us to tune out the static of everyday hassles and channel more positive energy.

The shadow box pictured here, created by artist Renee Troy, houses mementos and reminders of thankfulness. You can adapt this concept to any special holiday or event in your life; for example, for a birthday, you might include some ribbon from the wrapping paper, the barrette that your daughter wore, a flower from the centerpiece. Each item can go into a separate compartment.

Gratitude is an attitude that hooks us up to our source of supply. And the more grateful you are, the closer you become to your maker, to the architect of the universe, to the spiritual core of your being. It's a phenomenal lesson.

—**Bob Proctor**

Creating a Gratitude Vision Board

Many of you may already have gratitude journals that you keep daily or write in weekly. Some of you are aware of the power of keeping a list of things you are grateful for, and some vision board creators even add their updated gratefulness lists to their current vision boards. But there is great power in creating a gratitude board for your life.

Focusing on the Seven Wonders of Your Life

What Gratitude Really Means

Lee Brower, who appeared in *The Secret,* has created his own acrostic for the word "gratitude." He agreed to let me share it here:

Gift of giving

Remembrance of all that is good

A touchstone for global transformation

Transition to greatness

In acts of kindness

True wealth and abundance

Unyielding compassion

Divine clarity

Everlasting commitment to appreciation

Do you take time to appreciate the wonder of your own life? Are you grateful for this miracle called living? Many people ask me to analyze their vision boards and see what they can add that might be "missing" or that can make their boards serve them better. One of the most frequent items left out is thanks or gratitude for being alive!

A great way to inspire yourself is with the "7 Wonders" activity. Add it to your repertoire of weekly and monthly inspirational projects. The definition of "wonder" that applies best here is "to be filled with admiration, amazement, or awe; to marvel." List the seven wonders in your life. I'm not talking about material stuff but the states of being that inspire you, that give you a sense of purpose and meaning and bring joy.

Artist Shana Dressler, who created the "Seven Wonders of the World" vision board (page 125) affirms my belief that verbs move not only a sentence forward but our lives as well. Dressler's seven life wonders are all verbs. They include: to dream, to dance, to sing, to inspire, to explore, to love, and to serve.

What Are Your 7 Wonders?

Try to make a verbs-only list for a more Zen-like approach to looking beyond the stuff in your world! Use the phrase: I am grateful for the ability to _____.

Fill in the list below.

1. _____

2. _____

3. _____

4. _____

5. _____

6. _____

7. _____

Need help? My personal 7 wonders are: write, travel, play, vision, see, hear, discover. If you can't list seven, try starting with two or three. They might be: 1) practice the law of attraction; 2) be positive; 3) have an attitude of gratitude. See, it's getting easier by the minute.

Try repeating this exercise weekly, maybe on Sunday night before you start a new week.

7 Wonders Variations: Try these as well.

- List the 7 wonderful experiences you had last week.

- List 7 people you are grateful to have in your life.

- List 7 ways you are making a difference in the world.

7 Wonders of the World: The Art of Gratitude

To unlock some of the secrets to making a truly inspiring vision board that is also a work of personal art and truly meaningful to its creator, here's a more in-depth look at Shana Dressler's vision board. Dressler, a media producer, photographer, and future activist and philanthropist, shares her visions of gratitude and appreciation.

Overview: "I realize that what has stopped me from fulfilling my biggest dreams is that I have mastered the 'art of doing' but not 'the art of being,'" explains Dressler. She knows that it is in the being not just the doing that the law of attraction is activated.

For Dressler, her vision board—or wisdom collage, as she likes to call it—combines what I call defining images that represent personal core values and strong "power" visuals that function as her power words. Her vision statement is expressed in the idea of the "7 Wonders of the World," which is multitiered in its visioning of her life now and in the future.

Defining images: Dressler explains that the "OM" symbol in the center of the flower is a reminder that all types of energy have one factor in common: they vibrate. OM is also the eternal name of the Absolute consciousness, "I am," and it may also stand in grateful tribute to Dressler's own increasing sense of being centered.

Dressler's vision board also features images of deities and magical characters from popular literature. It incorporates one of her favorite images, Ganesh, the Hindu elephant-headed god who is known as the Remover of Obstacles. For Dressler, there is dual symbolism in the Ganesh picture, because she is grateful that now she is gaining some traction on a multimedia project she is developing entitled "Discovering Ganesh."

Next step beyond the board: Is it any wonder that these visions of appreciation and gratitude serve as a prelude for the next step in Dressler's life? She explains that she is now bringing together a community of doers and givers (activists and philanthropists) as she creates a new organization called NYC Giving Circle.

Shana Dressler calls this her "wisdom collage," and it serves not only as an inspiration and overview board but as a strong expression of gratitude for how far she has come in life and how far she is going on her journey as a practitioner of the law of attraction.

Using Your Vision Board to Express Gratitude

What if you already have an overview vision board but don't have time to create a special gratitude vision board? How can you use your current board as an inspirational reminder to express your gratitude throughout the day? Here are four options that I recommend to my clients:

✦ **Morning Gratitudes:** Stand in front of your vision board each morning after you brush your teeth and simply say, "I am grateful for this glorious new day." Then you can walk through the defining images and power words on your board and use them as a guide for your morning gratitude mantra; for example, look at the images on the board and experience them as if you already have them or are them. Look at the pictures that symbolize your new relationship and say, "I am grateful that I am in the right relationship." Focus on the image of the new house and say "I am grateful for my current living situation and for the new house I have, or something better." Be sure to add "or something better" because, according to Dr. Michael Beckwith, founder of the Agape Spiritual Center, there may be something better that the universe has in mind for you.

✦ **Coffee-break Gratefulness:** Either at work or at home, return to your vision board or a visual reminder of your board that you create at work, which might be one of the pictures from your board that you have

Giraffe: This image is about grounded vision. For Dressler, the giraffe image reminds her to be grateful for finally being grounded and viewing her life with an increasingly expansive vision. For someone else, a picture of a giraffe may simply be a reminder to be grateful for the courage to "stick your neck out." Dressler adds an image within an image so that even the length of the neck and the colors add another layer of gratitude for a life filled with energy.

Female matador: This is a defining image, which for Dressler is a reminder to be grateful for such traits as independence, boldness, and fearlessness. Dressler says, "On an archetypal level the female matador also reminds me to operate from a higher state of consciousness other than my ego."

Wedding henna, woman in racecar, and dancing couple: These images may be unexpected additions to a gratitude vision board made by a forty-one-year-old happily single woman, but Dressler is now grateful for the realization that she's ready to meet her life partner with whom to continue on life's journey. You can be grateful not just for what you have now but for the clarity of your vision for tomorrow. Now that's an amazing idea: being happy for what good will come tomorrow because, after all, the future is created now.

reprinted and placed in a frame on your desk or a facsimile vision board that you create on your desktop. Take a sip of tea or coffee or a refreshing glass of water, and say "I am grateful for this water, which refreshes me. I am grateful for this break, which is a reminder of how I am taking time to enjoy my life from this moment on." Then focus on your board itself or the visual reminder of your board, noting something specific on it; for example, "I am grateful for my upcoming trip to see the Taj Mahal."

✦ **Grace with Lunch:** Be sure to carry a small visual reminder of gratitude in your wallet or scan a few images into your mobile phone so you can easily click to them after lunch. At lunchtime, say thanks to your creative power, the universe, or God, whichever fits your spiritual practice. Saying grace at mealtimes is a practice many of us learned as kids at home or in

Artist Amber Coffey gives tribute to G. K. Chesterton's quote in her vision of gratitude displayed here. Coffey adds something special to each one of her creations, infusing her artwork with love and healing Reiki energy, an ancient technique for stress reduction and relaxation.

Gratitude is happiness doubled by wonder.

religious classes but later lost touch with in our busy lives. As an added benefit, many of my clients say that by beginning to say grace before meals they pay better attention to what and how they eat.

After lunch, don't forget to look at your defining images, or vision board if you're at home, to say your thanks again. If you carry your pictures with you or add them to your mobile displays, share them with a supporter. I often share my pictures with the barrista at my local coffee shop or with my favorite waitress. Many people are aware of the law of attraction, and by sharing your thanks you encourage them to go after their own visions.

✦ **Counting Blessings at the End of the Day:** A fun after-school activity or post-dinner ritual to begin is to literally count your blessings every day. Create a gratitude circle by holding hands—you can stand or sit cross-legged in front of your fireplace or look at your vision board or a defining image of a sunset, Buddha, or favorite family photo. Have each person say what he or she is grateful for that day. Each person can give thanks for something great that happened to or for him or her or can be grateful for good health or for just being home after coming in from a rainstorm. Some families make this into a game to see who can be grateful for the most things that day; the winner gets a symbol of gratefulness, like a gratitude stone or a symbolic gold-star paperweight to put on his or her nightstand. Then the object is recycled to others the next evening.

Mid-Afternoon Thankfulness Stretch

Just as at a ballgame, we all need a good seventh-inning stretch during the day. Make a commitment to yourself to take a break at some point during the afternoon and say thanks for your body and the power of your mind each afternoon.

Some of my clients actually take a short walk at 4 p.m. each day to keep them away from the candy machine and to literally stretch their gratefulness-reminder muscles. If it's raining outside, be thankful for the rain, which is reviving the flowers. If it's snowing, be thankful for this season of opportunity. Improvise. At the very least, set a time each day to get up from your desk.

Moms and dads might take time to color each day with their kids or to savor the recent drawings their children have created that are posted on the refrigerator; family members can say thanks as they look at each person in the picture. And, of course, add thanks for the other important family members not pictured, such as grandparents and aunt, uncles, and cousins.

Expressing Gratitude in Other Ways

Vision boards are an especially powerful way to express and focus on gratitude. There are some other great ways to do this as well. Visual reminders, such as those that follow, help keep all of us on track, just like road signs on the highway.

Creating a Virtual Gratitude Vision Board

Justin Whitaker created a virtual gratitude vision board on his desk by arranging real-life "versions" of his power words and values. Note that the paper-clip chain is arranged in the circular symbol of gratitude. The coins represent abundance; the pictures represent family, love, and future travel; and the Buddha serves not only as inspiration but as a reminder of gratefulness. You can set up a similar desktop or shelf at your office or anywhere in your house as a reminder to be grateful. No words are necessary. Its subtlety will be meaningful to you alone. It reminds me of office or ancient home altars, but these serve as visual reminders or defining images rather than tributes to deities.

Lee Brower's Gratitude Rocks

In the movie *The Secret*, Lee Brower, founder of the Brower Quadrant and the Quadrant Living Experience, shared the story of how his practice of carrying what he called a gratitude rock began to spread positive vibrations around the world and helped instill in him an attitude of gratitude.

In a podcast interview with Brower, I was surprised to hear there was even more of a story than that conveyed in the movie. During a difficult period in Brower's family life, he was taking a walk and found a rock and stuck it in his pocket. Right there, he made the decision that every time he touched the rock, he'd think of something he was grateful for and every evening when he emptied his pockets he would do the same.

When a man from South Africa saw him drop the rock and asked Brower about it, Brower explained his newly adopted habit to this man, who started calling it a "gratitude rock." Two weeks later, Brower received an email from the man explaining that his son was dying from a rare kind of hepatitis; he wondered if Brower would send him three gratitude rocks. Brower says, "Remember, these were just rocks off of the street, but I decided that I had to make sure that the ones I sent to him were special, so I went out to the stream and picked the right rocks and sent them off."

The man spread Brower's attitude of gratitude further. Four or five months later, Brower received another email from the South African man, who wrote, "My son's better. He's doing terrific." It continued, "But you need to know something. We've sold over a thousand rocks at ten dollars apiece as Gratitude Rocks, and we've raised all this money for charity."

Words of Gratitude

When you're holding your own Gratitude Rock, Brower recommends that you say a phrase such as "Every day . . . I choose to be in an attitude of gratitude. I get to choose how each day begins and receive the positive energy that accompanies my awareness of and gratitude for all of the many blessings in my life."

Special-Event Gratitude

Using vision boards or boxes to celebrate special occasions—graduations, birthdays, or anniversaries, among others—is a great idea. Following are examples of some of the special days in your life that you may want to celebrate by creating your own gratitude vision board or box. Many families are adopting an attitude of gratitude and creating Thanksgiving vision boards annually to celebrate that special day when all generations gather together.

- ✦ **Retirement Party:** Colleagues can each include one memento for the guest of honor.

- ✦ **Anniversary:** Include special souvenirs from trips, parts of favorite cards, or even exotic stamps from love letters sent from abroad.

- ✦ **Valentine's Day:** A candy heart with the words "Be Mine" can be complemented by the fortune from a cookie at a favorite Chinese diner. Include a favorite earring or cufflink, even though the other may have been lost. Add a newspaper horoscope for each of you, and note your partner's wonders by printing them on sticky notes or small adhesive labels and then decorating with glitter or glue-on stars and shiny hearts.

- ✦ **Wedding Shower:** A board or box can hold well wishes from each attendee and maybe flowers from the garden where the party is being held. An engraved coaster or a napkin holder might be incorporated as well. Don't forget to include pictures of the bride- and groom-to-be and a picture of the engagement ring itself!

- ✦ **Thanksgiving:** After eating dinner, you and your extended family can use snapshots from the day and vintage photos from old albums to create a gratitude vision board or box. Everyone can write what he or she is grateful for either on the board or on slips of paper that can be stored in a box.

This board was created by artist Annie Kaycora for a Halloween event, Scare for a Cure, that raises money for cancer-related charities. Vision boards like this can be created for any holiday to raise money for or support a favorite charity.

Gratitude and Sharing

You know my spin on the law of attraction triad of Ask, Believe, and Receive and my belief that creating and manifesting your visions begins with gratitude and is complemented by being ready to release the old and receive the new now, acknowledging your progress and asking for answers, and being your authentic self and believing you are deserving. GRABS isn't complete until you share. Sharing should become a focal point of your life and even your life's mission.

Community of Sharing

The vision boards in this section are examples of how my clients and colleagues share their talents and beliefs to support nonprofit or community organizations that they founded or for which they are spokespeople.

(below) *My colleague Tess Cacciatore's nonprofit World Trust Foundation strives to empower youths to become a global community, to create a connection for open communication and collaboration, to collectively eliminate racial intolerance, and to maintain a community of powerful and positive young people. Her vision statement is "Ignite, Empower, Unite," which you can see spelled out on her vision board. The board itself spotlights this by placing the statement at center stage on the top of the design. Pictures and original cartoons designed by Cacciatore complement images of kids around the world who share in the vision to create community and collaboration and eliminate racial intolerance. These images also reflect the international nature of this community. Cacciatore has designed a complete line of children's books and dolls called Bella Wishes (see the image in the lower left-hand corner of the board) and a portion of the proceeds from these creative concerns are given to the foundation.*

(opposite top) *Late-night TV sexologist and best-selling author Dr. Susan Block's philosophy of the Bonobo Way of Peace through Pleasure is inspired by the "Make Love Not War" bonobo chimpanzees, and her Block Bonobo Foundation is dedicated to protecting, promoting, and researching these amazing apes. She is grateful that, despite their grave endangerment, wild bonobos still exist and we have time to save them from extinction.*

(opposite bottom) *Janyse Jaud creator of* The Magic of Think, *a CD to help kids build self-esteem, is grateful for voiceover roles in "My Little Pony," "Strawberry Shortcake," and "Ed Edd n Eddy." Janyse's biggest thrill was meeting kids from the Make-A-Wish Foundation who came to see her and the crew in the studio.*

When Gratitude Is Hard to Find

While surfing the sections on gratitude and vision boards on Oprah.com, I was struck by one poignant but angry comment by a reader who was expressing how tough it is to find something to be grateful for and to vision beyond the day-to-day challenges of her family life in a trailer park. She challenged readers to be grateful when their food budgets were $40 per week—not enough to feed the family. I wondered how I could inspire people like her in this chapter.

There must be some inspirational story that might encourage the woman. So I used my favorite search engine and found this amazing true-life story of Cheri Haug from Wisconsin.

After seeing the "Law of Attraction" episode on *Oprah*, Cheri was inspired to create a complete line of Gratitude Bracelets. Haug has manifested many wonderful things in her life owing to her willingness to be grateful for the things she has. She lived in a mobile home for ten years. Whenever people asked her whether she'd prefer to live in a "real" house, she would tell them she preferred her trailer. The mobile home was affordable and allowed her to live rather cheaply while she launched her bead store business. Eventually the success of the store enabled her to buy a house. She recently sold the store to devote more time to her web business and to painting. Every good thing that has come into her life she credits with her ability to be grateful for what is and to visualize what might be

(opposite top) *Gratitude flows everywhere if you look on the positive side of life. Gratitude Bracelets created by artist Cheri Haug are available online. Haug's Gratitude Bracelets serve as visual reminders of how you can turn a negative to a positive and live a charmed life even if the going seems rough now.*

(opposite bottom): *Vision board creator Irena Makarchuk founded the nonprofit Harmony4kidz.org to help homeless children in New York City. Her group organizes celebrity concerts to raise funds for outreach programs. Makarchuk created this board in gratitude of her successful transition from engineer/inventor to songwriter/performer, so it offers double gratitude for her personal achievement and for the success of Harmony4kidz.*

ABUNDANCE

WELLNESS

LIVING IN

A.W.E.

ENLIGHTENMENT

WEALTH AND WELL-BEING

Is your path to live a life of wealth and well-being
all of the time, from this day forward? Sound like pie
in the sky? It's not! In this chapter, you'll discover
inspirational stories and tips from experts and regular
people that will help you create vision boards that
lead to abundance and prosperity and will serve you
in your quest for the best.

"To your health, wealth, and happiness" is one of my favorite toasts at
celebrations like weddings, birthdays, anniversaries and, of course, New
Year's Eve. Yet, I find that many people postpone and even refuse to
experience happiness and a sense of abundance until they reach their next
goal, get that next raise or meet that special someone. For them true joy is
elusive—always beyond their grasp. Most of my clients spend more time
worrying about what *might* happen in the future than being grateful for
the present.

Too many of us latch on to the drama of what's wrong versus celebrating
what's right in our life story as it unfolds. Others have long ago turned

Living in A.W.E.—abundance, well-being, and enlightenment—is your birthright. This vision board
for a sustainable community of that name is the creation of internet guru Mark Chasan, founder
of emusic.com, who now envisions eco-communities based on A.W.E.

the reigns of our future over to fate or to a partner or parent. Creating a wealth and well-being board and practicing abundance reminds us that we are our own destiny.

As we get older, we grow wiser and realize that life doesn't miraculously change once the next goal is attained. James Ray, author of the book *Harmonic Wealth* and one of the teachers in *The Secret* reinforces my belief when he writes that "the difference comes in the *attitude* with which you do things. When true happiness and fulfillment is reached, you'll learn that the journey is the adventure, the excitement and the fun of life!"

When you're in a rut, sometimes it's easy to forget that all you have to do to change your life for the better is to change your mind-set. The advice I offer my clients who are saddled with stuck-in-the-mud thinking is that "One door closes and another opens—but it's hell in the hallway, so, get out quick!" The best way to do this is with my GRABS formula.

Use the GRABS formula to reboot yourself each day. Remember to express **gratitude** for what you have; **release** the old ideas and be ready to **receive** the new; **acknowledge** your progress and **ask** for guidance and for what you want; **be** your authentic self and **believe** you have already received despite any obstacles or challenges; and **share** your bounty.

Artist Theda Sandiford's colorful collage reminds us that everything we need is always ours to have—the piggybank of life's treasures is limitless! Embrace change!

Enter paradise... the Gate Is Open for You!

I received a simple yet profound email, which reminded me of what's possible, and what exists right now and that we're just not acknowledging. When the going gets rough, and the bills pour in, we forget the value of the limitless "spiritual currency" within us all!

"The funny thing is that in spite of the euphoria one feels upon entering paradise, cloaked in miracles, surrounded by angels, love, and unimaginable beauty, it gradually becomes all, you know, commonplace, ordinary, and then, shockingly... invisible. Yep, I'm talking about life on earth."—Note from The Universe, aka Mike Dooley, teacher in *The Secret*.

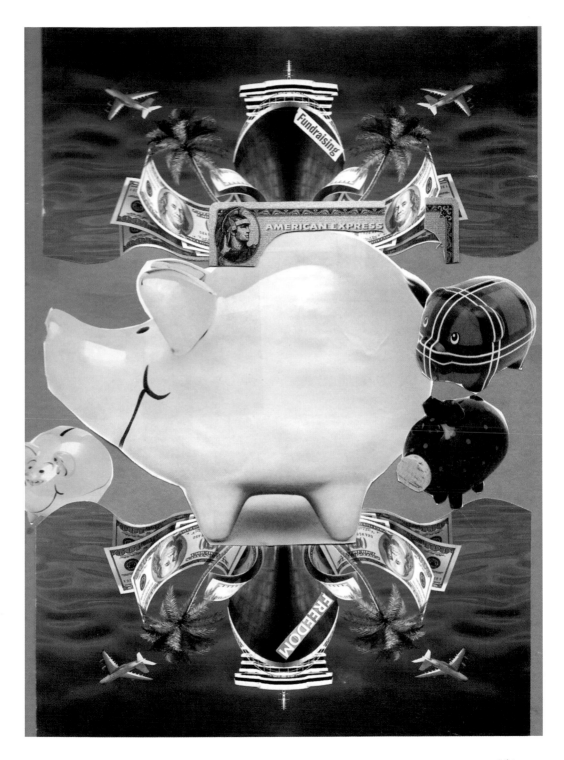

(right) Never set an alarm clock again—now that's the life. Millionaire Mommy Next Door Jen shares her vision board and her recipe for prosperity and success in an online blog. She even donates the proceeds to charity. It's great to see that her board celebrates some of the priceless things in life like chasing fireflies, discovery, and fun.

(middle) Evelyn Lim is a life coach from Singapore who writes inspiring articles. She reminds us with her vision to be grateful for all aspects of our lives including love, happiness, peace of mind, and family with heart.

(bottom) Cornelis Boertjens, creator of the Orange Peel Vision Boards, shows us that even grown boys can vision the best toys. His board features a Porsche Carrera 4S and a Audi Q7 and a boat, reminding us that there's plenty of abundance and we deserve the best in life.

7 Tips to a Life of Wealth and Well-Being

These tips will help you experience the abundance life has to offer.

#1: Get in as close proximity as possible to your vision.

How can you be a publisher of a newspaper if you don't have the capital? By bootstrapping it—parlaying revenues from ads from one week to print the paper the next, according to Diane Boone, editor and publisher of *Melanian News*. She was recently featured in a national story that saluted her for "going for it" and creating one of the top niche publications in the media business. She is living the vision on her board today.

Attracting national news about her publication Melanian News *instills even more confidence in Diane Boone that she is living her vision. Being close to her dream was not enough, she actually created the specialty publication herself and got major promotion for her ongoing success as a female publisher.*

#2 Share Your Vision—and the Creation of It—and It Will Grow to Fruition!

Longtime colleague and former client Richard Harris reveals when he was designing his "Seeds of Life" vision board at a weekend retreat he was overprotective of his supplies—his picture, his scissors, and his ideas. It wasn't until he spotted an image he wanted in another person's stack of magazines that he realized sharing is caring and it was a way of completing his own vision board. "Somehow I kept thinking my old magazines were too valuable to share. Only to realize that sharing brought me an experience and a collage that was invaluable!"

#3 Getting Is Giving

Getting by giving isn't just trendy, it adds up to great business dollars and sense! Cynthia Kersey, author and founder of Unstoppable Enterprises, shares the amazing tale of how she turned a broken heart after her marriage dissolved into a dream come true for families in a distant land.

Richard Harris's collage shows how he is balancing body and spirit by combining marathon running, music, and a loving relationship with his wife Mary, with ongoing spiritual practice.

Phoenix *is an amazing piece by Max Gold, who created this "fusian art" to symbolize his own rise from a relationship he had to release. Like Cynthia Kersey he found a greater purpose to fill a great pain. Gold, who was once homeless, now enjoys national prominence and prosperity by sharing his creations that are amazingly simple and amazingly complex at the same time—not unlike our lives and the map to our own dreams come true. Gold's work blends digital art, hand painting, and spirituality and provides a whole gallery of what may just be inspirational for your own defining image.*

Kersey was devastated by her divorce after twenty years of marriage and was feeling sorry for herself as she sat in her parents' house over the holidays with her young son. She remembers thinking, I can't control what happened here but I can control how I respond, so next holiday I'm going to do something for someone else! She turned to her mentor Millard Fuller, founder of Habitat for Humanity, for advice and he told her about the needy in Nepal. She thought it sounded like an opportunity to give to others.

Kersey agrees with me and many wise leaders that if you have a great pain in your life, you need a greater purpose. She asked herself how many houses she would need to build to offset the pain and came up with one hundred. During the next year, she wrote a book and while speaking about and selling it, she raised enough money to build that number of houses. She actually made more money during that year than she had ever made in a year.

#4 Embrace Change
It is the only constant and by releasing your concern or by following the advice that my mentor Susan Jeffers embraces "to feel the fear and do it anyway" you realize the opportunity to live life to the fullest.

#5 Be a Star in Your Own Life
Rewrite your life script. We are all special. We are all actually made from the same elements as the stars in the sky; in other words, we are "star stuff." We can change our lives completely if we want--we just need to believe in ourselves and our abilities.

#6 Matchmake for Success
Put people not just places and things on your vision board, and ask a mentor, pal, or colleague or coach to introduce you to these VIPs for possible joint ventures or for pitching your own services, or just for inspiration! Ariane de Bonvoisin, founder and CEO of First30Days.com, raised five million dollars for the launch of the First30days Change Network using her vision board, a guide to a who's who of people she wanted to meet for her new business venture and book.

#7 Get a Life, Not Just a Job
Have your board's image reflect the importance of relaxing, enjoying, and living (see image opposite top).

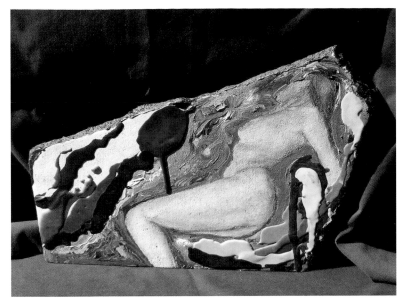

(left) *This defining image by international artist Pablo Solomon has a title that says it all,* Mellow Yellow.

(below) *Ariane de Bonvoisin is* a big believer in vision boards, and check out all of the VIPs on hers. Discover the *who of your* how *by asking a mentor, coach, or colleague to "matchmake" you with leaders you'd love to meet to guide you on your path to success.*

Social Entrepreneurship

Social entrepreneurs, as defined by Ashoka.org, one of the first non-profit groups to pave the way for social entrepreneurism, are individuals with innovative solutions to society's most pressing social problems. Rather than leaving societal needs to government or business sectors, social entrepreneurs solve problems by changing the system, spreading the solution, and persuading entire societies to take new leaps.

Social entrepreneurs identify resources where people only see problems. They view the villagers as the solution, not the passive beneficiary. They begin with the assumption of competence and unleash resources in the communities they're serving."

—**David Bornstein, author of**
How to Change the World: Social Entrepreneurs and the Power of New Ideas

It can take many forms but sometimes it is cause-related, such as my past client Candy Lightner's founding of Mother's Against Drunk Driving (MADD); sometimes it can involve actual donations to worthy nonprofits or emerging countries.

For two decades now I've been a believer in multiple streams of income that evolve from public/private/non-profit partnerships. Through the success of my experiences I've discovered the value of being a social entrepreneur who not only creates prosperity for myself but is a catalyst for the abundance of others. It's not enough to contribute to the system when there is opportunity to create the new (showing people how to fish is always better in the long run than just selling fish because the village, not just the person, benefits). Sometimes people ask me what my secret formula is. So for the first time I'm revealing the analogy to my vision map to success.

Cynthia Lynn attributes her vision board and her daily journal for the lightning speed at which the vision that she and her mother shared—to fund the building of the Schumo Center for Well-Being at Albright College in honor of Cynthia's father—was actualized. She explains that the process from vision to reality took less than two years.

Vision Map to Success

Organize a visionary team that is interested in venturing into unknown forests to source hidden trees of prosperity.

> *Delve into*
>
> *Multiple streams of initiative*
>
> *Multiple streams of income*
>
> *Multiple streams of inspiration*
>
> *Multiple streams of innovation*
>
> *Multiple streams of improvement*
>
> *That flow into rivers of opportunity that flow upstream into mountains of success.*

The following is an example of social entrepreneurship and one of my visions that came true and is now an example of opportunity world-wide.

Vision Behind the Missing Kids on the Milk Cartons Campaign

About twenty years ago I was consulting for a major ad agency and we had an opportunity to pitch some community promotion programs for Ralphs Grocery Store chain, part of Kroger Co., to extend their TV and ad messages to new audiences.

In doing my research for the presentation to Ralphs, I saw a small article in a regional newspaper about a little dairy in Michigan that was doing something unusual with its milk cartons—it was actually picturing images of missing children from a government database on the side of its cartons. It just struck me as brilliant.

Beloved, I pray that you may prosper in all things and be in health, just as your soul prospers.

—New Testament: 3 John 1:2

Ralphs actually produced its own milk cartons, not just a few thousand like the Michigan company but hundreds of thousands of cartons. I figured this idea of trying to find missing children, which was a major social issue two decades ago, before the Internet, other media, and later the National Center for Missing & Exploited Children got involved, had the potential to be a win-win situation for my client and gain goodwill from consumers and at the same time benefit society at large. During the meeting with Patrick Collins, president of Ralphs, I pulled out the clipping and laid it on his desk. Before I had a chance to speak, he opened his drawer, pulled out the same clipping, and asked how much money we needed. I said $100,000; my client was just mesmerized—no other word for it. Then and there the president wrote a check for $50,000, gave it to my client, and said "Let Joyce run with this."

Three weeks later I had the cast of a hit TV show at the time, *Hill Street Blues*, behind it and had convinced then-California assemblyman Gray Davis (who later became governor of the state) to introduce a bill in Sacramento championing the cause of missing kids and extending the picture campaign beyond milk cartons to billboards, bus stops, and other public spaces. I even wrote the child safety tips for the milk cartons myself—making it the center of many family mealtime conversations and garnering headlines and press support regionally and nationally as other firms adopted similar programs.

The defining image for that public-private social entrepreneur venture was of course that small newspaper clipping. The Who of the How was the president of Ralphs, and the Why was to benefit all kids and provide a showcase for the future of community involvement later leading to the Amber Alerts for missing kids and other community awareness programs. The vision extended from milk cartons produced by a small dairy in Michigan to the country as a whole and throughout the world. By sharing your vision with others you'll see how the circle of giving grows exponentially when the timing is right.

The Wellness Revolution

If you look more closely at the opening concept vision board for A.W.E. created by my client Mark Chasan and his partner Allison "Freddie" LeBlanc, you'll see that they can serve as role models for all of us as we head into what is now becoming known as the wellness revolution.

Choose Boundless Living

Well-being is a lifestyle that goes beyond images on your vision board of the guy with the six-pack abdomen or the gal with the glowing skin. Bob Doyle, one of the teachers featured in the movie *The Secret*, the creator of Boundless Living, and an internationally respected fitness expert, told me that great health really is your choice. He explains, "I started it like most people do, and you learn techniques like writing lists or cutting out pictures; all of these things are designed to change your emotional state and get you into vibrational resonance with what you want." Today he shares his discoveries in an online program called The Boundless Living Challenge, a free, innovative online event designed to help people move off of their couches. Doyle's program is a great opportunity to realize your visions of health and wellness and like many online resources can be super-charged when you add the power of a custom-designed vision board to the process.

Vision a World of Health and Wellness Abundance

As many of you venture out of your corporate worlds into the new age of owning your own businesses, freelance work, or creating multiple streams of income, you'll be inspired by this role model, vision board creator Melissa Stone. Once a finance executive at a sportswear firm, life took a turn and she found herself and her child homeless. Her vision to change her own life for the better is helping others reach their own wellness goals through yoga, body treatments, and even the fun of belly dancing.

Stone shared four specific manifestations of her board (not shown here): 1) The classes she is now offering at a studio; 2) the local talk show she hosted for almost a year on radio; 3) the new inspirational and meditation DVD and CDs she now plays during classes and sells as an additional revenue source; and 4) her articles for *Belly Dance Magazine*.

Health and Well-Being Are Priceless

"The greatest wealth is health" is a slogan that dates back to the Roman Empire and the philosopher Virgil, who once studied medicine. Today, great health and well-being may be even more precious. But many of us are caught up in the numbers game—what the scale says, how high our cholesterol is, if we can control our blood pressure. Here's a great example of how a vision board can lead you to overall well-being and finally release excess weight and worry.

(opposite) Who says a business plan has to be boring? When it's created by Jennifer Lee from Artizen Coaching and is right-brained, meaning it is "thinking outside of the box," it can be fun and interactive, just like your new idea for delving into the wellness economy and making a splash!

(below) Shelly Fitzsimmons, certified fitness trainer, expresses her passion for helping and guiding others to excellence by creating a vision board featuring bold affirmations and inspiring real-life photos. Wellness, spirituality, and health all stress-free—what a combination!

Releasing 100 Pounds: Vision Boards and Weight Management

Donna Kozik is frank about recounting her own challenge with weight. Just days after celebrating a sixty-pound weight loss when she was twenty-four years old, her dad died of a heart attack. She turned to food to dull the pain and grief, reaching an all-time high of 345 pounds. She yearned for a fresh start but was still eating. After moving to San Diego from Pennsylvania, she began to feel like her weight was stifling her inner spirit, "I wanted to do so much but I was exhausted." During her prayer group one night, she asked her friends to send her a solution and soon after the spiritually based program "The Road Less Traveled with Food" came into her life showing her how to stop overeating once and for all.

"Overeating was only half the battle," Kozik explains. What she needed was a vision to pull her. Kozik created a vision board that included these elements: Slender women who were glowing with good health, an affirmation card that declared, "I choose to be happy," and lots of beautiful fruits and vegetables.

"It's kind of like a high five for what I've already achieved," says Kozik. She still works with that same board and just keeps updating it.

Vision Boards and Weight Loss

Here's how a vision board can help you lose weight:

✦ It helps you keep your attention on what you want and not what you don't.

✦ It reminds you that no matter what else is happening in your life—happiness is always your choice.

✦ By keeping your vision board front and center it reminds you that you're striving along the path to your vision.

(top right) *Many people make vision boards for greater health—creating one for weight loss lets you get even more specific in determining "what you want." Donna Kozik says if the photo or word is something you strive for and makes you feel fabulous, include it!*

(bottom right) *Eat, drink and be mindful . . . You read it right! Dr. Susan Albers, clinical psychologist and author of* Eating Mindfully: How to End Mindless Eating and Develop a Balanced Relationship with Food, *believes that we all deserve what she calls "mindful eating," so much so that she's created her own spin on the age-old adage of eat, drink, and be merry. Here she shares a vision board that hints at some of the hallmarks of mindful eating. She encourages her clients to create mindful eating boards like this one to help them reach their goals.*

I Deserve...

Mindful Eating

To eat "real" food in moderation & guilt free (no pseudo food—non organic, processed, or diet food)

To make each bite a mindful bite.

To sit down and relax while I eat...

To be at home in my own body. Tuning into myself to really know my hunger and fullness.

To enjoy food like a child...

Out with Weight Loss and in with . . . Weight Donation or Weight Reduction. Discover the Power of HUNA!

In a recent podcast with Dr. Matthew B. James, I discovered the option of not focusing on losing weight but rather considering "weight donation" or "weight reduction." Dr. James, chair of the Assn. for Integrative Psychology in Hawaii, has trained thousands of people to use the principles of Huna to manage health, wealth, and love. Huna is a western label given to Hawaiian ancient healing and spiritual shamanism.

Dr. James used these Hawaiian ancient principles and is now seventy pounds lighter and twenty million dollars richer. How did he do it? James explains that Huna teaches that words don't just *describe* our reality but they actually *create* our reality.

Want to "attract" less weight? Dr. James says shift what you say. "I stopped calling it weight loss, because when you lose something you go look for it. Changing your words changes your thinking and *that* will change your actions." He urges us to no longer say we want weight loss, because we really don't want to find it again, do we?

New labels better suited to optimal health are "weight donation" or "weight reduction." James explains, "Your body's energy levels can be enhanced or depleted by your choice of words. Donating feels good, so say that—it gives you energy. After all, someone, somewhere in the universe could use a little extra weight. So, donate it and reduce it!"

By shifting your thinking about something as simple as a word, you can increase your level of energy and then your effective action. People who practice Huna create total flexibility of the mind, body, and spirit. It's a secret practice of many famous teachers we all respect.

Artist Jennifer Perry-Haught added decorative stickers to one of her original paintings to create an inspirational vision for herself and her son who lives with a painful health disorder. Flowers, butterfly, heart symbols, and animal totems all encourage her on her life journey.

157

CASE STUDY:

When Your Vision Is Life-Saving

A vision board served Jackie Olson when her son was diagnosed with autism, and it led to an even closer relationship with her husband and a family that today is filled with joy.

How Olson's vision board served her in dealing with her son's diagnosis of autism is an inspirational story and shows how invaluable a health vision board is for your family's well-being.

Olson explains that she used visioning techniques and a vision board as both a source of inspiration and to find the right path to find the help she needed for her son and the family. "At first I was angry at the world, at God, at everyone and everything," she remembers, thinking back to the time four years prior when she found out about the diagnosis of autism. Instead of being overwhelmed by the options for treatment, she created a vision board to guide her. She even wrote optimistically, "I have the perfect and right therapies for my son."

Envisioning Health and Happiness

Olson and her husband spent time each evening visualizing health and happiness for their son and in turn reached a new level of happiness together as a couple and as new parents. Her vision of finding the right source for assistance with their son's care and growth was realized when Olson met Britt Collins, an intern working on her occupational therapy license. Collins evaluated their son and was the first to realize he had what's called sensory processing disorder; he was not only non-verbal but couldn't wear clothes or even be at family events. In those days her son had to put his head to the ground to see his toys because he couldn't focus standing up. Today the couple is thrilled that their son's occupational therapy has worked so well. He is happy and can be in a mainstream class.

Olson and her husband realize that occupational therapy is not a cure for autism, nor do all kids respond the way their son did. But they do know that therapy helped them.

A vision board served Jackie Olson when her son was diagnosed with autism, and it led to an even closer relationship with her husband and a family that today is filled with joy. She shares her story here and on an inspirational DVD she produced with the therapist who turned out to be the who of her how.

She says, "The vision boards helped in every aspect of our lives. I am healthier than I've ever been. My husband feels better than he ever has. We're financially better off than we ever were, and we're emotionally happier. We're in what I call the life flow and it's good."

Here's how the Olsons used the techniques featured in this book:

+ **Defining Image:** A boy jumping off a dock into water. Joy and happiness.

+ **Vision Statement:** They keep their thoughts on peace, love, health, wealth, and happiness.

+ **Vision Board:** Olson adds a sophisticated spin to her boards by putting them on canvas and featuring them as art around the house. "The vision boards are a 24/7 lifestyle for us. We love them!"

+ **Visioning:** She's uses guided imagery, a version of visioning that guides your imagination toward a relaxed, focused state.

How the Olson family lives the Law of Attraction GRABS formula:

+ **Gratitude:** She explains that they were always grateful for their son and she has a mantra from Dr. Beckwith's Agape community on one wall that she refers to daily: "I am grateful, so thankful. I am one with the spirit all around me, and truly appreciate each day with my son and what his journey with autism has taught me as a person. My priorities are different, my world is different. I vision helping more people. I want to give and to serve others in a way that I never imagined. I trust that whatever happens with my son, he'll have a good life."

+ **Release and Receive:** In creating her board originally, Jackie realized she had to release her feelings of hopelessness and be open to new therapies. The boards help the Olsons focus on what they want and what is truly important, and allow them to receive what they are ready for. Jackie explains, "Everything else falls away."

+ **Ask and Acknowledge:** The Olsons acknowledged that they were seeking a *how*, and through inspired action and asking for assistance they found their *how* in the *who* of a dedicated therapist.

+ **Be and Believe:** Being true to your inner beliefs is crucial when the challenge seems insolvable. The Olsons believe 100 percent in themselves and their visions. They know that they can create the positive.

+ **Share:** As her son entered mainstream kindergarten, Olson cried tears of joy knowing that he was going to be okay. Instantly she decided to share and give back and produce a DVD on occupational therapy and autism. The family donates a portion of the DVD sales to the L.A. Autism Walk and even sponsors other events with the National Autism Association and TACA (Talk about Curing Autism).

The Olsons' advice: Practice patience in seeking solutions to health and life issues. Be sure to let negativity roll off your back and don't give it or anyone toxic any attention. Choose happiness.

Finding Your Fountain of Youth

Just feeling good is not enough for many of us anymore. We share the quest for eternal youth or at least the goal of feeling younger than we are. According to Bob Doyle, "the fountain of youth is being able to feel that sense of exuberance for the duration of your life. You can always feel young. You have the choice to feel youthful for as long as you live. The more you feel youthful, the longer you probably will live." Doyle explains that the fountain of youth is really a matter of looking at what wealth means to you; what health means to you; what youth means to you. Does it mean you have a ton of energy and you're out playing every day? Doyle and other health leaders agree with me that you make the choice of what inspires you to feel young, to resonate with youth and the newness of life rather than living in the past and complaining about today!

Health has translated into wealth for model #18 Marisa Petroro on NBC's popular game show "Deal or No Deal." Petroro is a survivor of sarcoma and her current goal is to pay tribute to the hospitals and doctors who helped her fight the disease by raising one million dollars toward research and a cure. A vision board makes a perfect visioning poster for your own favorite health and wellness charity. Petroro embellished her board with symbols of angels and flowers and brilliant hues of oranges and gold that complement the sparkly gowns she wears on the show.

Personal Empowerment

The most important change in the wellness movement has been "personal empowerment" of the individual. You not only take responsibility for your health and fighting "dis-ease" but are active in going beyond just setting up a fitness program to embracing wellness as a way of life.

Imaging Health and Wellness

Mainstream Health Community Embracing Vision Boards

I've been surprised by the response from medical professionals including doctors, who recognize the power of vision boards. According to Dr. Steven Hodes, a traditionally trained doctor whose approach to well-being includes both scientific and spiritual causes for health issues, "Self-awareness precedes self-healing. We need to actively participate in the process of discovering the underlying metaphysical basis of reality. We can then proceed to participate in our own journey toward healing."

This doesn't have to be a challenge. When you're selecting pictures and visuals for your own "well-being" vision board, check the range of designs that these artists selected for inspiration on your own creations. Delores Burgess's highly personalized vision board touts powerful images that remind her of how successful she's been in fighting breast cancer and how much she wants to encourage other women to take charge of their greatest asset in life—their health—through her ongoing seminars and an upcoming one-woman musical show on the West Coast that will travel across country.

(opposite bottom) *The creator of this vision board, Delores Burgess, believes that "she who has health has hope." A breast cancer survivor, this singer, author and speaker empowers women to be proactive and to take control of their health. Those "pink" boxing gloves may make an appearance in her one-woman show.*

Soul portrait . . . going beyond the board. Artist Jennet Inglis uses the seven colors of our planet's electromagnetic color spectrum with the color magenta on a quantum dark field. Her "soul portraits" are variations of vision and dream boards used in art therapy. She created her first one as a healing tool when the call came to help a friend's child who was catatonic with clinical depression. Take a note from Inglis and consider creating a vision board that has a dark background and brilliant colors when you really want to reinforce your desire for health, wealth, or happiness. Consider sharing your newfound talents in vision board creation with those not as fortunate as you.

Vision Journals

Try a variation of a vision board called a vision journal. You may choose to envision your life of well-being by using pictures only or you may want to start a written journal as well. Check the tips here from *Journalution* author and advisor Sandy Grason.

I realized how complementary Grason's campaign to get millions of people to journal is to mine with vision boards. Grason defines "journalution" as "the act of revealing your inner wisdom through writing." I asked her to provide advice about why you might want to use a journal after you have created your vision board, and she explains that:

- ✦ a journal will keep you on track;

- ✦ a journal is there to remind you of your greatness;

- ✦ a journal and a pen are some of the best tools for creating a map of the life of your dreams; and

- ✦ a journal can serve as a call to the universe to bring all of those dreams to life.

Grason shares my belief and that of other wisdom leaders in this book when she says, "The real journey happens within" and adds "there is always an internal shift that comes before you see your vision manifest in the outside world."

(opposite top) *Jodee Bock turns her "goal cards" into a deck of reminders she can carry with her. Easy to slip a few spare ones in for jotting down your journal notes on the run! You could even glue on a mini-version of your vision board too! Soon there will be mobile versions of vision boards and defining visuals you'll be able to thumbclick up on your iPhone or other mobile device. These are great reminders about exercise, eating tips, and even funny jokes or affirmations you want to share with friends.*

(opposite bottom, right) *This page in Cynthia Lynn's Vision Journal reminds her to focus and tend to specifics but also to live "crazy time"—outside the box—and to be grateful for her roots.*

(opposite bottom, far right) *Good vibrations can just as easily come from the view from your home as the view from an exotic beach. Cynthia Lynn's journal page reminds us all to reach our arms out as infants do and say YES to others, life, and ourselves.*

Reintroduce the word "zing" to your vocabulary.

happy to nap

Life's a roller coaster . . . enjoy the ride.

FRANCK MULLER
GENÈVE
CRAZY HOURS

Finalize LIS Foundation Business Plan with Diane . . . and meet with Les, Frank, Andrea, Sal, Bill, Brad, Mike 12/16

Make Christmas special for as many people as possible

Finalize Estate Matters: IRS debacle, Stowe component, Trust funding, TW piece . . . and meet with Mike and Brad 12/16 at 2:00

A VIRTUOSO OF ENOUGHNESS

pleasures intense

Where those who've got it, go.

live without the worry

Live the Emotion

pamper.

"Relaxing the mind and nurturing the body produces visible beauty from within."

Bubble Bath

Because not everyone lives to collect air miles.

Good Vibrations

Out with Resolutions, in with Vision Boards!

If you are starting fresh, whether it's a new year or just a new life you yearn for, don't make a resolution but make a vision board instead.

As mentioned previously in the book, the start of every season is an ideal time to "re-vision" your life. But I also believe that you can use more traditional dates as a lift-off point for your new vision, just add a new spin to those old traditions this coming year. Instead of New Year's resolutions, create a "new you" vision board or a "New Year vision challenge" for yourself. Here are some sample boards that other colleagues and clients have created to focus on their own fitness and well-being plan throughout the year:

Happiness Boards

Having fun and being happy is an important key to wellness, and a dose of gratitude and thanks is always welcome—even if the appreciation comes from you, to you.

Choosing Happiness

Laughter Is the Best Medicine

While it is normally only considered cliché that "laughter is the best medicine," specific medical theories attribute improved health, increased life expectancy, and overall improved well-being to laughter.

Eva Gregory, co-author of *Life Lessons for Mastering the Law of Attraction*, part of the Chicken Soup for the Soul series by Jack Canfield and Mark Victor Hansen, is probably better known as Coach Eva. She is now recognized as one of the creators of International Happiness Day, on July 10 each year. Why did she found the event? Coach Eva explains, "Choosing happiness is your birthright! The reason we want to be, do, or have anything in our lives is because we think it will make us happy! So what if you chose to be happy now? The interesting thing about that is once you choose to be happy all the things you want will begin to flow to you!

(left) *This collage of happily married couples is from the film* Project Everlasting *and accompanying book produced by Mathew Boggs and Jason Miller. The two bachelors traveled twelve thousand miles in search of America's greatest marriages. They believe that to experience any dream, you must first see it with clarity.*

(below) *Nick Thorsch, the creator of "The Ultimate Vision Board" Facebook application, envisions health, wealth, and happiness in his digital vision board.*

The Ultimate Vision Board
Directory Status: Approved
Your application is currently listed in the Application Directory. You can edit or delete your entry.

Daily Active Users	About Page Fans	Total Users
10,000	100,000	1,000,000

ABUNDANCE

Jack Canfield

cocreator of
Chicken Soup for the Soul®
with Janet Switzer

The Success Principles

How to Get from
Where You Are to
Where You Want to Be

I am joyfully celebrating the sale of one million copies of The Success Principles.

A digital vision board is a dynamic addition to your desktop or laptop screen. You can even carry a version on your mobile. Take a peek at Jack Canfield's vision board here, which features images of abundance. Don't stop now—check out Jack's 5 steps to take next in this special afterword included for readers.

Jack Canfield Shares
the Six Steps to Take Next: Dream Big and
Continue to Envision Your Success

By Jack Canfield, founder and CEO,
Chicken Soup for the Soul Enterprises, Inc.

Don't stop now. Continue to write down and talk about what you do want, not what you don't. Remember: be as specific as possible. Then practice these six steps every day and encourage your family and friends to join in on the journey to success.

1. *Every morning: release and visualize.*

   Every morning take five minutes to focus your mind on your desires, goals, and intentions. You may want to begin by facing your vision board for inspiration. Relax, close your eyes, and visualize your desires and goals as already being fulfilled. Release any negative limiting beliefs. Don't fight or argue with the thought, just release it. Spend thirty seconds to a minute on each of your core desires. Focus on feeling as if you are already manifesting your desires in life; the intensity of that inner feeling is what fuels the attraction to you.

2. *Continue to use external images to focus on your desires and goals.*

   Throughout the day keep focused on what you want to manifest by surrounding yourself with visual images of the things and experiences you want to attract into your life. When you look at any of these pictures, do what Bob Doyle, who is featured in *The Secret* teaches: Think the thought, This is mine now! This is who I am!

3. *Think a Better Feeling Thought.*

   Throughout your day, pay special attention to when you feel disappointment, resentment, frustration, or anger about your experiences. Remember, it's your feelings (which are created by your thoughts, opinions, and beliefs) that are attracting your current circumstances. Consciously make a vibrational shift by changing your thoughts to ones that make you feel better. Focus on thoughts that bring you joy (your lover, your best friend, your grandchildren, your favorite vacation spot) and take action by doing the things you love (petting your cat, working in your garden, listening to your favorite music). Encourage your spouse, your children, and your colleagues to join you in this exercise.

4. *Practice an attitude of gratitude.*

Focus on all of the things in your life (most of which you take for granted) that you are grateful for—your health, your children, your job, the nice weather, electricity, running water, a nice sound system, your flower garden, your pets, and your friends. Share this practice with your children and colleagues. Record what you are grateful for in a gratitude journal. You might want to consider keeping two journals, one for business and one for family.

5. *Take action.*

Here are two different ways to take action: through obvious actions like test-driving the exact model car you yearn for and arranging for automatic withdrawal from your checking account of 10 percent of your weekly income to a special "car savings account." Be open to inspired action when the universe begins to respond to your obvious actions by sending people, resources, and opportunities to manifest your desired goal. As you begin to have inspired ideas, act on them. Follow the gentle proddings; often your intuitive impulses may lead you to a path of wonderful fulfillment. Are you going in the right direction? If you're feeling joy, you are on the right path. Follow your joy!

6. *Acknowledge that it is working.*

Start to look for signs that your life is changing for the better. Be sure to appreciate these changes. When you find the perfect parking space, acknowledge it. When you get the table you want in a restaurant, acknowledge it. When you receive unexpected income, acknowledge it. When you meet someone who can help you achieve your goal, acknowledge that the law of attraction is working. The more you acknowledge, the more it will work.

If you want to know what you are thinking about, notice the results you are producing in your life. To change those results, change your vibration by changing your thoughts and feelings.

Note from Joyce:

Try some of the valuable tools in Jack Canfield's new DreamBig™ Collection. They complement this book and expand on my beliefs with proven techniques for applying the law of attraction to your own life. You'll even discover how to create your own dream list and what to write in your gratitude journal. Check out the valuable tips for getting your children, teens, and whole family involved. Go to: *www.ihaveavision.org/dreambig*

ACKNOWLEDGMENTS

Thank you to Marta Schooler, publisher of Collins Design, and her team; to my amazing agent Irene Goodman; to all the contributors and artists; and to my mom and dad, brother Frank, and my Aunt Hilda. With special thanks to Elaine Palmer, PK Fields, Lynn Eisenberg, Lisa Osbourne, Pamela Harris, Susan Levin, Paula Correia, Annie Kaycora and Marilen McIntyre, Bart Wallace, Jan Tuck, and my pals down the hall: Ella, Terry, Sarah, Diane, and Bob. With appreciation to longtime supporters Richard and Mary Harris. Props to my Vision Board Creators Meet-Up Group, especially Suzanne, who helped with proofreading, and Jerry's Deli for hosting us! Special tribute to my colleagues Robbie Motter at NAFE and June Davidson at ASLA. Applause and a thousand apologies to the many other VIPs, contributors, and artists who, alas, were not included because of technical, time, or space limitations but will be featured on www.ihaveavision.org with podcasts and interviews, including Margaret Beck, Dan Hollings, Noah St. John, Karen Joyce, Marsha Malka, Beate Chelette, Hale Dwoskin, Jim Driscoll, Ruben Gonzalez, Randy Gardner, Jim Bunch, Lynn Andrews, David Lander (Squiggy), Christopher Lowell, Judith Parker Harris, Scott Ryan, and too many others to even mention here!

A million thanks to Cornelis Boertjens and his wife Linda for their support and contributions from the start of this project. A tribute to Joe Heller—without your irresistible offer we might not see this book. To my longtime colleague and one of my own gurus, Karen Stricholm, for her fabulous input. To all the PR people who went above and beyond the call of duty including Michelle Tennant, Kate Romero, and John Stellar, and to all those who responded to Peter Shankman's HARO note. Appreciation to Dawn Anfuso for early input and advice.

Thanks in advance to all of you who join in sharing the vision of this book, especially the dozens of launch partners such as Eons.com, First30days.com, Amazing Woman's Day, NAFE.com, VacationVocations.com, ExquisiteSafaris.com, American Seminar Leaders Assn. (ASLA.com), CEOSPACE.biz, Kimmierose.com, Sedona.com (The Sedona Method), MarieDiamond.com, and many more including many of the teachers of the Law of Attraction and other wisdom leaders and speakers and authors. To all of you who are joining me as the first worldwide Certified Vision Board Consultants as we create abundance and share our gratitude around the globe and beyond!

CONTRIBUTOR CREDITS AND RESOURCES

Cover: Art by Mary Anne Erickson, www.maryanneerickson.com

Art by Katy Taylor, www.KatyTaylor.com

Page ii: Donna Factor

Pages vii–ix: Bob Proctor, www.bobproctor.com

Page xiii: Mai-Liis Chaska Peacock, www.NewPathwaysHealing.com

Chapter 1: Visioning

Chapter opener: Art by Rochelle Schofield

Page 2 (left): Photo by Bettina Koelle, www.worldbank.org

Page 2 (right): Photo by Bob Kudlay, bkudlay@yahoo.com

Page 3: Contributor, Dr. Michael Bernard Beckwith, www.agapelive.com; thanks to Anita Rehker, editor

Page 3: Art by Michelle Oravitz, www.mystical-artist.com

Page 5: Art by Jennifer McLean, www.healingrelease.com

Page 7: Art by Katy Taylor, www.KatyTaylor.com

Page 11: Joe Vitale, www.mrfire.com

Page 11: Photos by Ben Mandel, www.imamerchant.org; art by Annie Kaycora, www.anniekaycora.com

Page 12: Contributor, Reverend Cynthia James, www.cynthiajames.net, www.milehichurch.org

Page 18: Art by Jamie Nast, author of Idea Mapping (IdeaMappingSuccess.com & IdeaMapping)

Page 19 (left): Art by Katy Taylor, www.katytaylor.com

Chapter 2: Your Personal Vision Statement

Chapter opener: Art by Mary Anne Erickson, www.maryanneerickson.com

Page 23: Photo of the Shroyer children by Keith and Susan Shroyer.

Pages 26 and 27: Art by Jennifer Lee, www.artizencoaching.com

Page 28: Photo by Amy Ho (originally posted on www.flickr.com)

Page 29: Art by Jessica Smith, from Australia

Page 39: Reference to The Broth, www.thebroth.com

Page 40 (top): Art by Akum Norder, www.momerath.etsy.com

Page 40 (bottom): Photo courtesy of Bill Richmond for GE, www.ge.com, and www.ymcasaratoga.org/firstnight

Page 41: Art courtesy of Judith Parker Harris, www.fromblockedtoblockbuster.com

Page 41: Art by Dave Pyke, courtesy of Eva Gregory, www.coacheva.com

Page 41: Art courtesy of Leigh Golterman, www.peaceplease.com

Chapter 3: Creating Vision Boards

Chapter opener: Art by Mary Anne Erickson, www.maryanneerickson.com

Page 46: Contributor, Aras Baskauskas, www.tundragear.com

Page 47: Art by Beverly Keaton-Smith

Page 49 (top): Art by Katy Taylor, www.katytaylor.com

Page 49 (bottom): Art by Monica Austin

Pages 50 and 51: Contributor and art, Lisa Osbourne, www.lisa.fm

Page 52: Art and digital vision board by Cornelis Boertjens, www.orangepeel.co.nz

Page 53 (top): Art by Edward Mills, www.edwardmills.com

Page 53 (bottom): Art by Bethann Shannon, www.fridainheaven.etsy.com

Page 56: Art by Theda Sandiford, www.misstheda.com

Page 58: Contributor, Mary Manin Morrissey, www.lifesoulutions.com

Page 59: Art by Lauren George

Page 60: Contributor Lee Brower, www.leebrower.com and www.quadrantliving.com

Page 61: Art by Parée Eagleton

Page 67: Art by Annie Kaycora, www.anniekaycora.com

Page 71: Art by Peggy S. Pirro, http://outofhandart.blogspot.com and http://crooked5280.blogspot.com

Chapter Four: Activating Your Vision Boards

Chapter opener: Art by Marsh Engle, www.amazingwomansday2008.com

Page 73: Quote: Mary Manin Morrissey, www.lifesoulutions.com

Page 75 (top): Art by Katy Taylor, www.katytaylor.com

Page 76 (bottom): Art and photograph by Kirsten Stokes, www.flickr.com/photos/salamandermediaworks

Page 76: Art by Aysha Griffin, www.ayshagriffin.com

Page 77: Art by Pamela Moss, www.innervisionportraits.com

Page 78: Scott Adams, www.dilbert.com/blog

Page 79: Learning Strategies Corp., www.learningstrategies.com

Page 80: Art by Joy P. Choquette, http://chicchickbiz.etsy.com

Page 81: Art by Theda Sandiford, www.misstheda.com

Page 82: Contributor, www.coping.org

Page 82: Art by Theda Sandiford, www.misstheda.com

Page 83: Contributor, www.coping.org

Page 84: Contributor, www.coping.org

Page 86: Art by Theda Sandiford, www.misstheda.com

Page 88 (top): Art by Katy Taylor, www.katytaylor.com

Page 88 (bottom): Art and photos courtesy of Aras Bauskauskas, www.tundragear.com

Page 89: Contributor, Marie Diamond, www.mariediamond.com

Page 90: Contributor, Marie Diamond, www.mariediamond.com

Page 91: Art by Annie Kaycora, www.anniekaycora.com

Chapter 5: Relationships

Chapter opener: Art by Pamela Moss, www.innervisionportraits.com

Pages 94–97: Contributor and art by Naava, www.naava.com

Page 99: Art by Jayne Pierce a.k.a. zJayne, http://zJayne.etsy.com

Pages 100 and 101: Contributors Andy Nicholson and Diane MacDowall, art by Andy Nicholson, www.executive-relationship-coaching.co.uk

Page 102 (top): Art by Max Gold, Father of Fusion Art, www.bymaxgold.com

Page 102 (bottom): Art by Diane MacDowall, www.executive-relationship-coaching.co.uk

Pages 103 and 104: Contributor Marie Diamond, www.mariediamond.com

Page 105: Art by Lynda Naranjo

Pages 106 and 107: Contributors and art, Judith Claire and Frank Wiegers, www.judithclairecounseling.com, www.topgunlove.com

Pages 108 and 109: Contributor, Jina Bacarr, www.jinabacarr.com

Page 110: Contributor and art, Renee Piane, www.rapiddating.com

Page 112: Art by Pamela Moss, www.innervisionportraits.com

Page 114: Art by Katy Taylor, www.katytaylor.com

Pages 115, 116, 117: Contributor and art, Linda Boertjens, www.visualizeyourgoals.com

Page 119: Art by Beth Greer and her daughter, www.supernaturalmom.com

Chapter 6: Gratitude

Chapter opener: Art by Renee Troy, www.reneetroyartonline.com/

Page 122: Contributor, Shana Dressler, www.shanadressler.com

Pages 124 and 125: Contributor and art, Shana Dressler, www.shanadressler.com

Page 126: Art by Shana Dressler, www.shanadressler.com

Chapter 7: Wealth and Well-Being

Page 145: Art by Max Gold, www.bymaxgold.com

Pages 146 and 147 (bottom): Contributor and art, Ariane de Bonvoisin, www.first30days.com

Page 147 (top): Art by Pablo Solomon, www.pablosolomon.com

Page 148: Definition by www.ashoka.org

Page 148: Quote by David Bornstein, www.howtochangetheworld.org

Page 149: Art by Cynthia Lynn

Page 151: Contributor Bob Doyle, www.boundlessliving.com and www.wealthbeyondreason.com

Page 152: Contributor, Melissa Stone, www.balancestudio.org

Page 152: Contributor and art, Jennifer Lee, www.artizencoaching.com

Page 153: Art by Shelly Fitzsimmons, www.shellyfitzsimmons.com

Page 154: Contributor, Donna Kozik, www.IcanStopovereating.com

Page 155 (top): Art by Donna Kozik/Marjorie Old, www.ICanStopOvereating.com

Page 155 (bottom): Contributor and art, Dr. Susan Albers, www.eatingmindfully.com

Page 156: Contributor, Dr. Matthew B. James, www.huna.com

Page 157: Art by Jennifer Perry-Haught

Pages 158 and 159: Contributor and art, Jackie Olson, www.TRPwellness.com

Page 160: Contributor, Jackie Olson, www.TRPwellness.com

Page 161: Contributor, Bob Doyle, www.boundlessliving.com and www.wealthbeyondreason.com

Page 161: Contributor and art by Marisa Petroro, www.marisapetroro.com Thanks to NBC for the use of Marisa's images and the famous million-dollar briefcase from "Deal or No Deal," www.nbc.com.

Page 163 (top): Art by Jennet Inglis, www.jennetinglis.com

Page 163 (bottom): Art by Delores Burgess

Page 164 Contributor, Sandy Grason, www.sandygrason.com

Page 165 (top): Art by Jodee Bock, www.jodeebock.com

Page 165 (bottom): Art by Cynthia Lynn

Page 166: Contributor Eva Gregory, www.coacheva.com

Page 167 (top): Contributors and art Mathew Boggs and Jason Miller, www.projecteverlasting.com

Page 167 (bottom): Art by Nick Thorsch, http://apps.facebook.com/ultimatevisionboard

Page 168: Cornelis Boertjens, www.orangepeel.co.nz

About the Featured Artists

Thank you to all the artists who contributed vision boards and defining images for the book. I am especially grateful to the artists whose visions could not be included because of technical issues with their high-resolution pictures or because of space limitations. I look forward to featuring many of you in the workbook that will follow.

A special note of gratitude to the following artists who contributed numerous vision boards, collages, and other original designs for this publication:

Mary Anne Erickson is a life-long painter, graphic artist, and co-owner of Blue Mountain Bistro Catering Co. and Bistro-to-Go with her husband Richard Erickson. She has been inspired by many teachers over the years and now has come to realize the greatest teachings present themselves in each moment. By declaring a strong intention and combining it with artistic vision, we can empower ourselves to create whatever we want in life! www.maryanneerickson.com

Annie Kaycora is an artist with a passion for performing arts and entrepreneurship. Having dipped her brush in dance and acting as well as business, she currently finds herself deeply involved with a multimedia spectacular, www.TheStarWalkers.com, both creatively and in management. She enjoys self-development books and has a strong spiritual connection with the Universe. Visit her at www.AnnieKaycora.com.

Pamela Moss is an artist, life coach, and collage vision workshop leader who creates unique "possibility portraits" for people who want to remember who they really are and to live intentionally. These portraits are heirloom works of art, painted in egg tempera and embossed gold leaf like Renaissance altarpieces; they celebrate individuals, couples, families, and close friends. Each portrait begins with a powerful conversation about what "lights you up," the gifts you've gotten from your challenges, and why you're here. See www.innervisionportraits.com.

Katy Taylor is a singer, a Riso-Hudson Enneagram teacher, an Interfaith Minister, and a lifelong spiritual seeker (the Diamond Approach). She does not identify herself as a visual "artist," per se, but loves to be involved with art in order to keep her creative, expressive, intuitive, passionate juices flowing. She is blessed to share her life with her partner Dave Hall, for whom she has created many collages. See www.KatyTaylor.com.

Theda Sandiford is an aficionado of both pop culture and technology. She has fused her interests to build an internet marketing and consulting firm (Theda Dotcom LLC) that creates unique content campaigns and develops marketing strategies for her clients, including Microsoft/Zune, Asylum Records, SOHH, Simmons Lathan. Theda also co-hosts weekly wine events in New York City with her wine-tasting networking group, SuperNodes, www.supernodes.blogspot.com/. She is also an avid photographer, mixed media artist, and blogger, www.misstheda.com.

ABOUT JOYCE SCHWARZ

www.ihaveavision.org, email: joyceschwarz@gmail.com

Joyce Schwarz is an author, a producer, and a Hollywood and VIP coach and dealmaker. She is also a social entrepreneur and founder of the Center for Successful Recareering. Originally from Cleveland, Ohio, she lives and works in Marina Del Rey, California.

Schwarz was one of the early women pioneers in multimedia and new media and has successfully launched more than 75 venture-funded start-up companies. She is an internationally recognized speaker, corporate advisor, and futurist. She combines more than 20 years in advertising for major agencies such as Foote Cone & Belding with a bachelor's degree in journalism from Ohio University and a master's degree in film from USC. She did MBA studies at the University of San Francisco.

"I created, wrote, and produced this book to fulfill my life's motto 'To Live the Possible Dream' and to continue to express my own vision statement 'To open doors for others and walk through them first.'" What started as a personal project expanded to become an open book with more than 75 wisdom leaders, best-selling authors, and VIPs contributing. Artist vision boards and defining images came in from around the world including dozens of states and scores of countries. Thanks to all of our partners who agree to continue to support this book and the future of vision boards. I am grateful to everyone involved in this project!

Book Website: To find out more about sharing your own vision and to hear podcasts and be part of a community of like-minded people who support your dreams, go to www.ihaveavision.org.

To follow the progress of this book and its supporting outreach campaign, go to the blog www.visionboard.info and the Joyce Schwarz blog on Amazon.com. Also check out our Facebook Official Vision Board group and the special app for creating vision boards on Facebook.

To access the website from your mobile use www.tinyurl.com/vision411

Notes

Notes

Notes

Notes

Notes

Notes

Notes

Notes

Notes